SHOW
BUSINESS

SHOW
BUSINESS

RON SCHRAMM

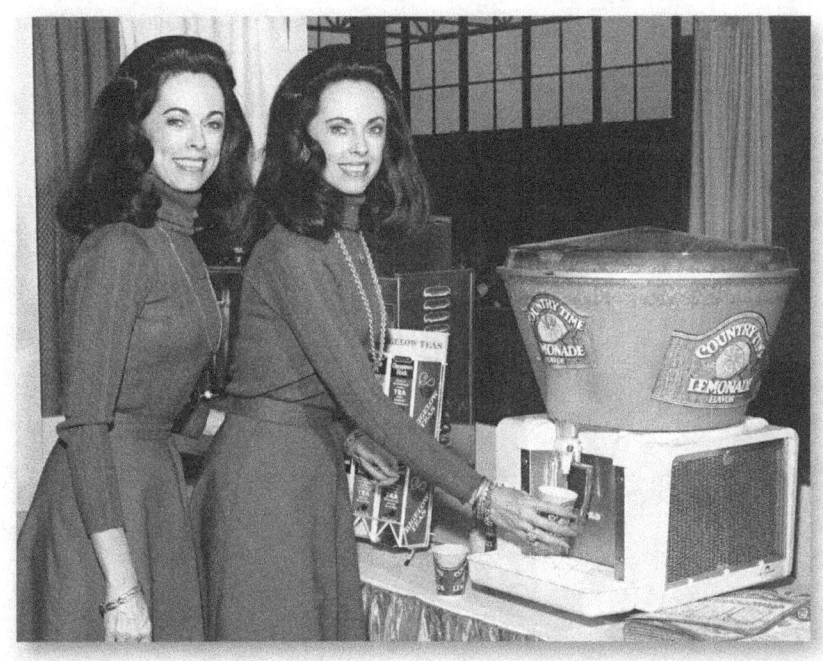

iUniverse, Inc.
Bloomington

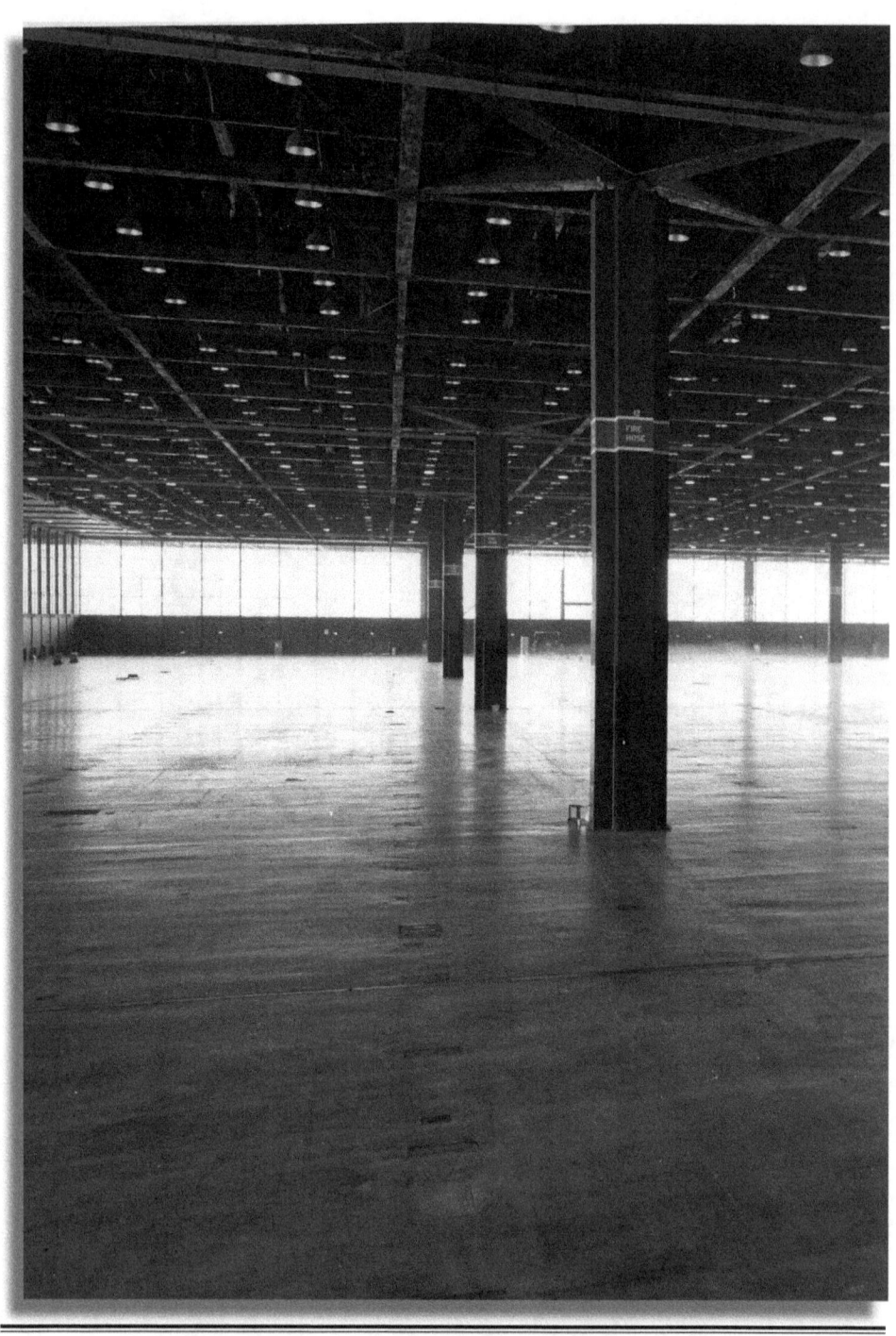

McCormick Place, resting between shows, 522,000 sq. ft.
of exhibition space, before the 3 additions added 2 million more.

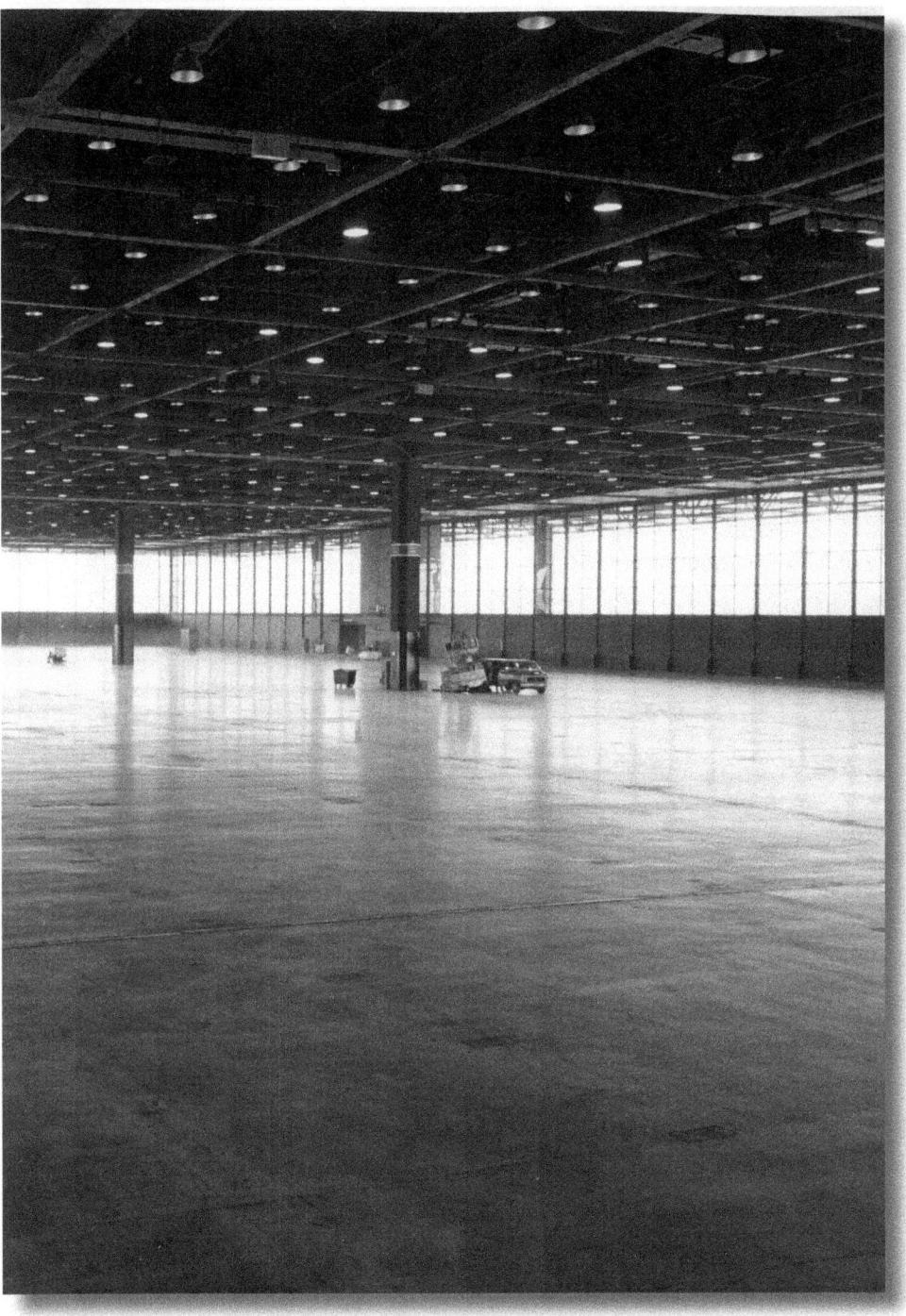

SHOW BUSINESS

iUniverse books may be ordered through booksellers or by contacting:

iUniverse
1663 Liberty Drive
Bloomington, IN 47403
www.iuniverse.com
1-800-Authors (1-800-288-4677)

ISBN: 978-1-4759-0290-7 (sc)
ISBN: 978-1-4759-0341-6 (hc)
ISBN: 978-1-4697-9849-3 (ebk)

Library of Congress Control Number: 2012905204

Printed in the United States of America

iUniverse rev. date: 10/16/2012

This book is about Show Business—the Trade shows held in giant venues like Chicago's McCormick Place, where American and foreign businesses display and sell their products. I have recorded what I think are iconic views of the marketing of these products to American businesses, and to America. Trade shows are at the marketing heart of American commerce, but these are often trade show views with a twist.

Some of my photos are classics: 20-foot-tall Coke™ bottles, big enough to quench America's thirst; a Chevy "Astro" van displayed by—who else?—beautiful women in spacesuits. Some are quite quirky: a giant scissors, deftly-captured, about to snip something at a ribbon-cutting ceremony; a beautiful woman—there are many of them here—driving a forklift in high heels. These trade shows are all about selling products but, when I've looked, I've often seen things in a different way.

Most of my photos were shot in the 1980s in McCormick Place, the largest convention center in the United States. The original building, with its prized site on Chicago's lakefront, is a modernist example of how Carl Sandburg's City of the Big Shoulders has transformed itself into the City of the Big Sellers. Recognize that Chicago's Marshall Fields building on State Street was once the largest store in the world. The Merchandise Mart, hulking over the Chicago River, is the world's largest commercial building. And the Sears Tower—built by the nation's largest retailer—was the tallest building in the world for 23 years. Chicago is clearly obsessed with selling, and selling big.

These images were photographed using black and white film in a Hasselblad Superwide camera. I am drawn to views that are clean, structural, and even rigid, which is why architect Gene Summers' original McCormick Place building—like a broad black slice of the great Midwestern Plain jutting out over Lake Michigan—is so attractive. In these photos, you will often see its internal starkness set off against the mayhem, the selling circus, going on below.

I suppose I should apologize here for the obvious objectification of the women who appear in these photos. I can only say: I took their pictures, I didn't place them in these shows. It is clear that these beautiful women are here selling forklifts and pipe connectors to attract the attention of the mostly male attendees at events like the International Machine Tool Show. But if you had to compare machine tools all week during your once-yearly business trip, wouldn't you appreciate a little softness among all that metal? The marketing may be crass, but it works.

Come with me into the world of Show Biz.

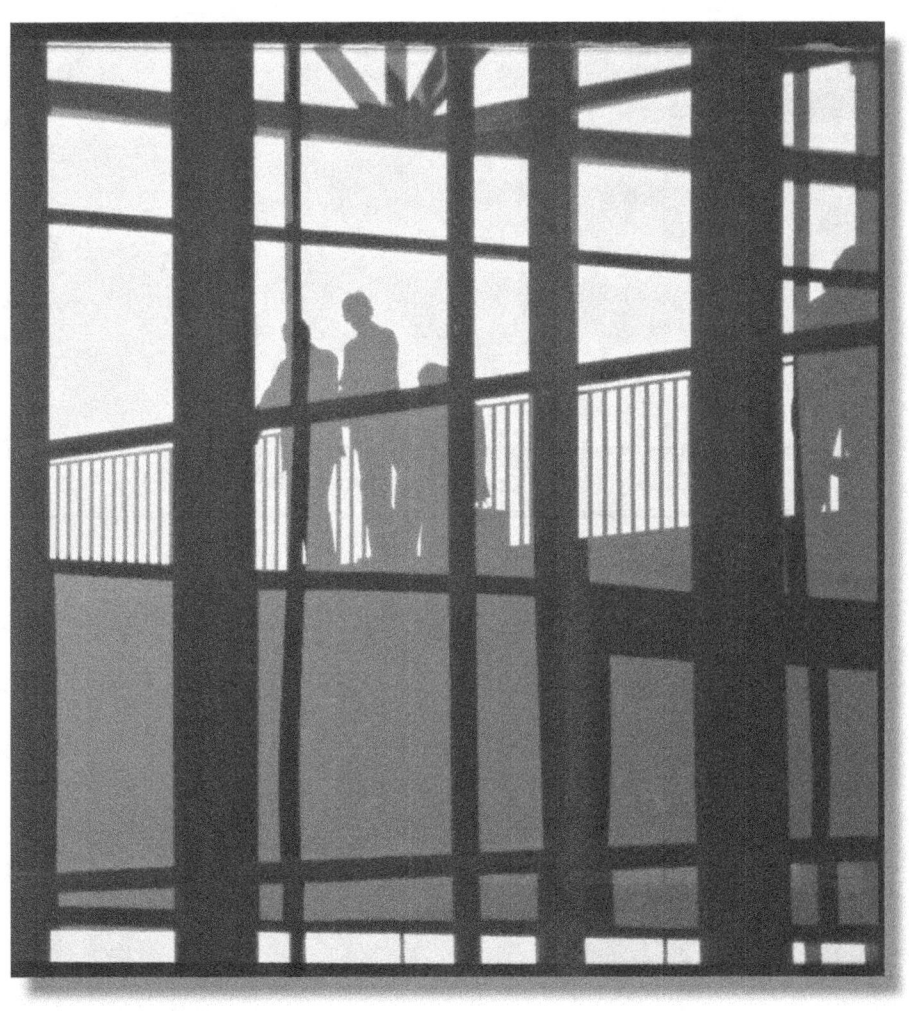

Show setting up, Apparel Mart, Ready

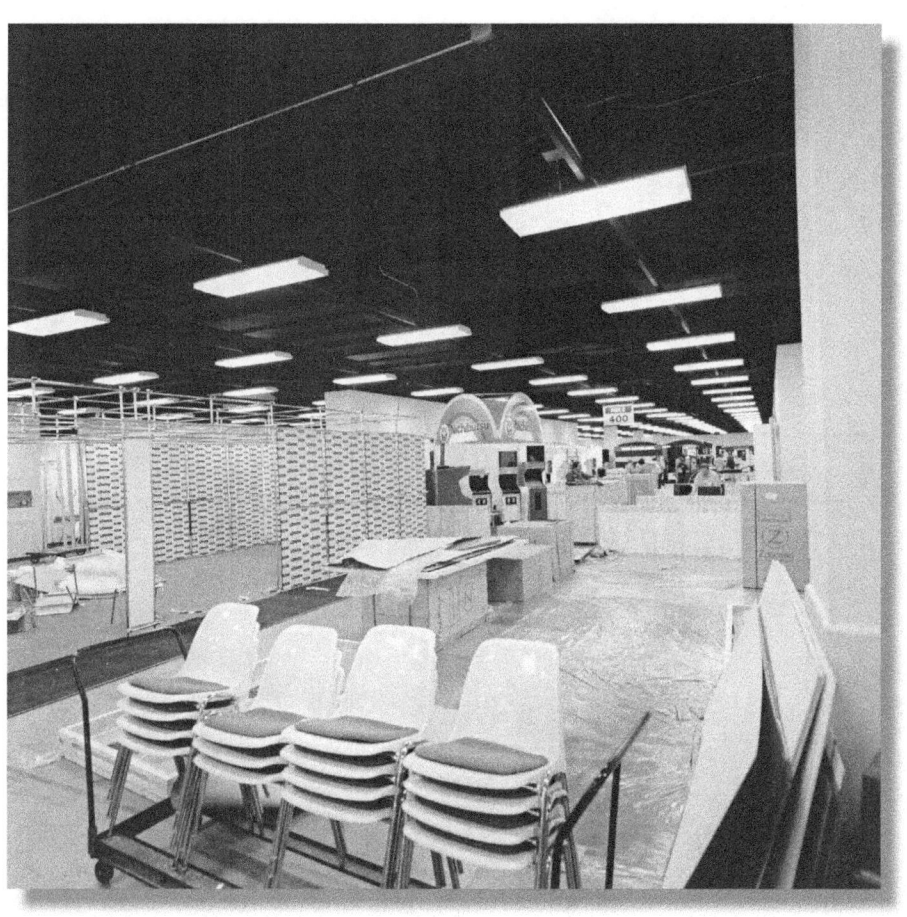

Set

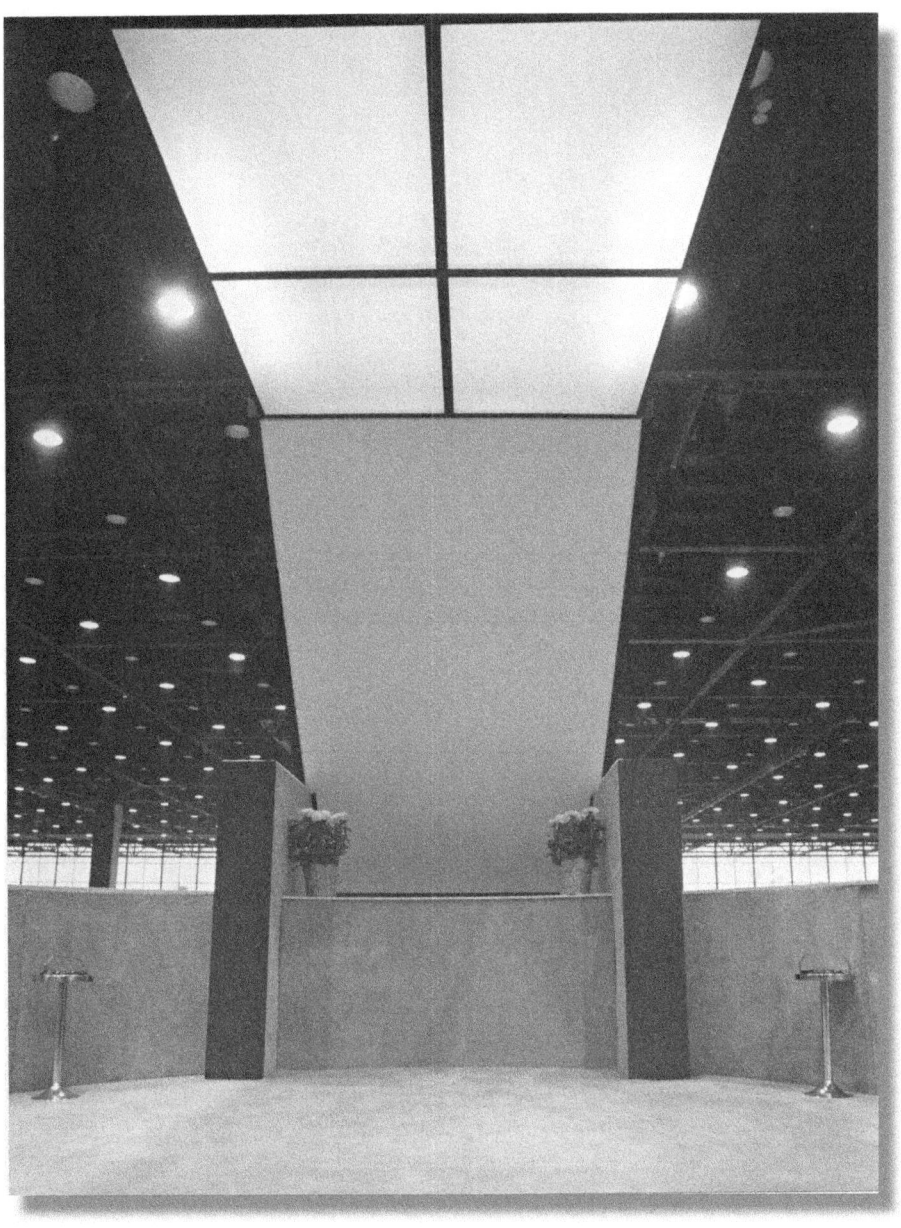

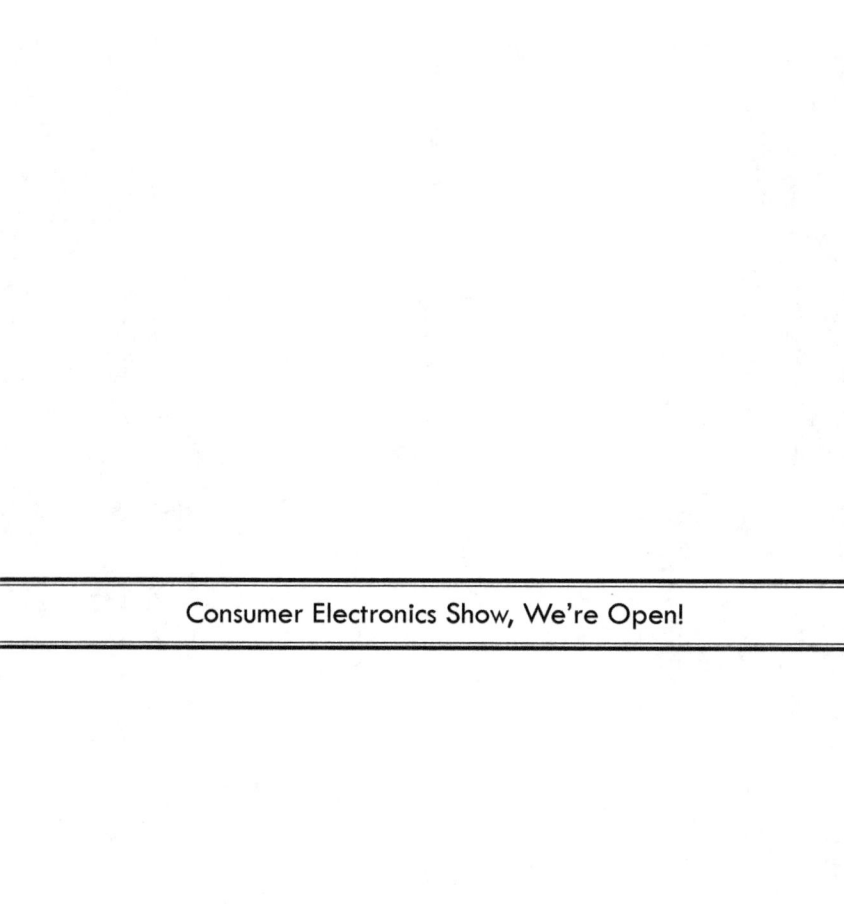

Consumer Electronics Show, We're Open!

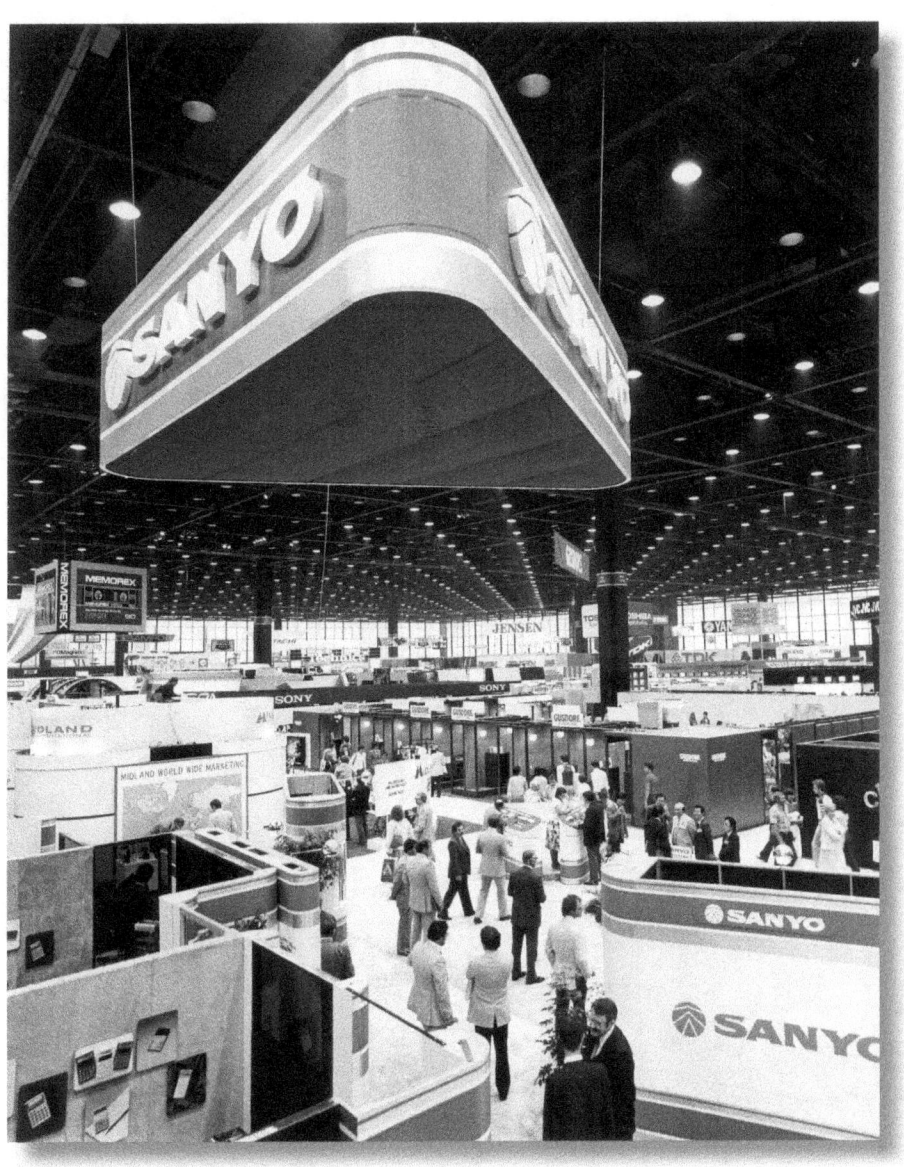

Sell!

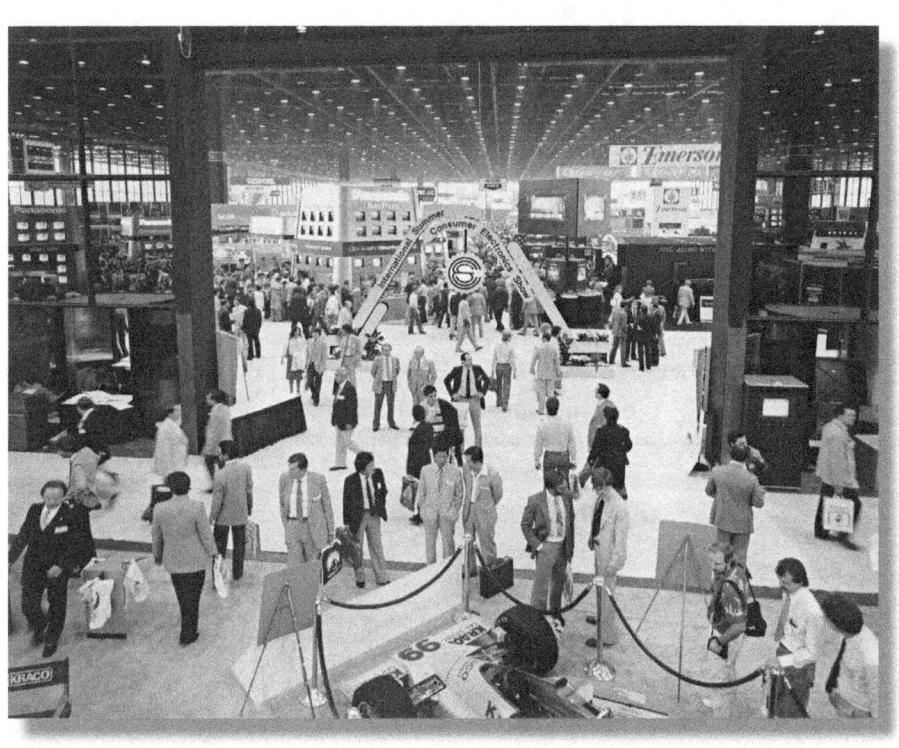

American Power Conference. Check out those grins.
These men think they hold the power.

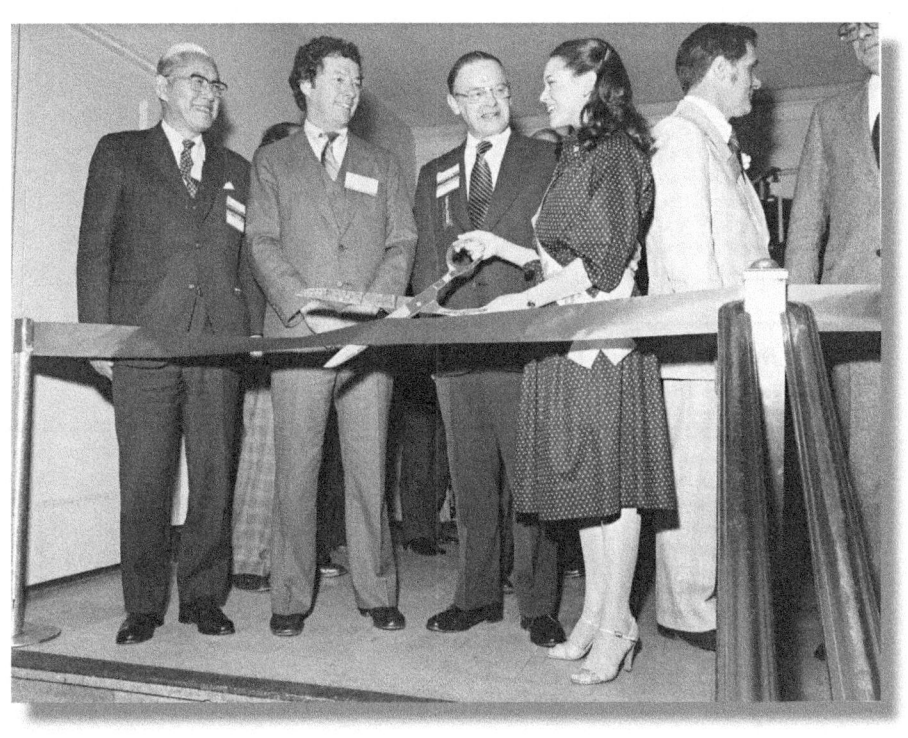

Mining Industry Institute. Put your shoes back on Honey, and we'll take this baby for a spin.

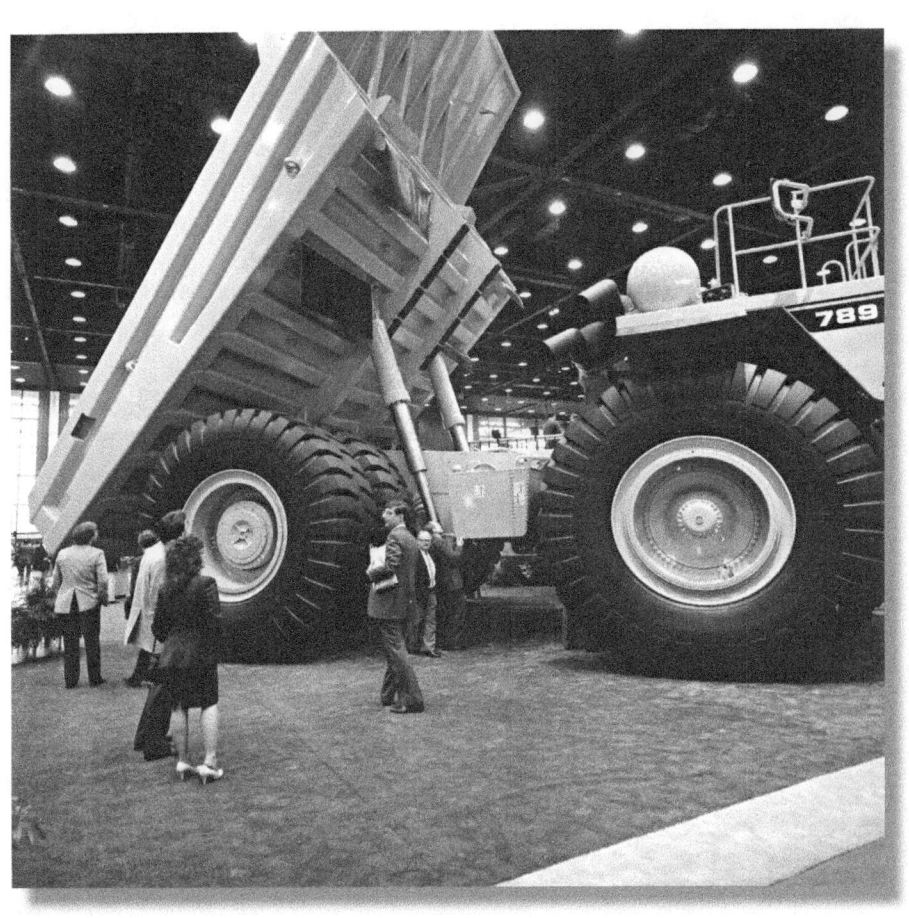

Midwest Auto Show. Astronauts 4 the Astro Van,
room for one lucky driver.

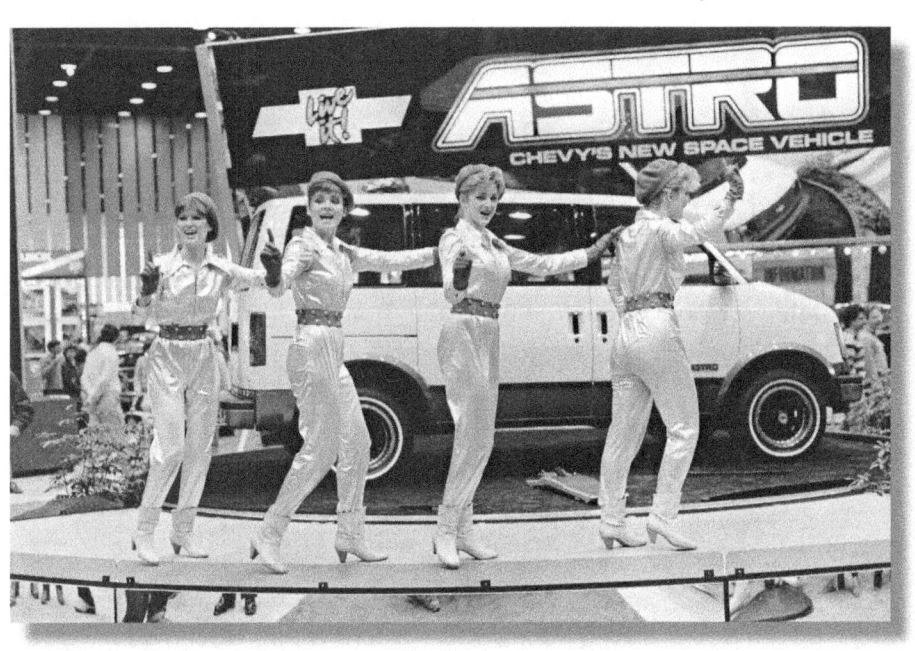

Midwest Auto Show. The Buick Questor. Cool car (never built).
How about that outfit?

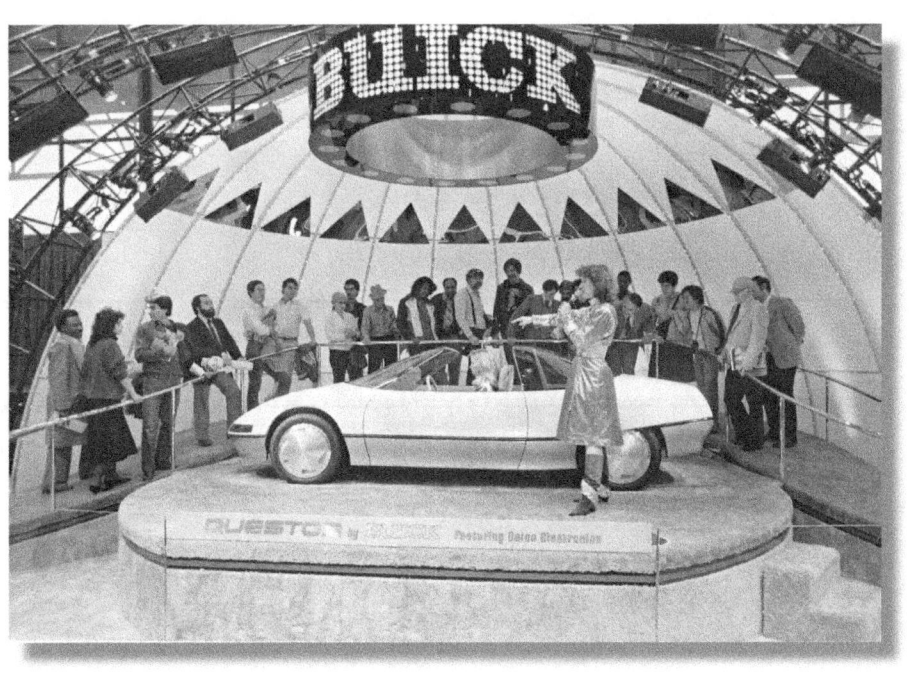

Midwest Auto Show. Direct from Stuttgart's famed test track
into Detroit's nightmare.

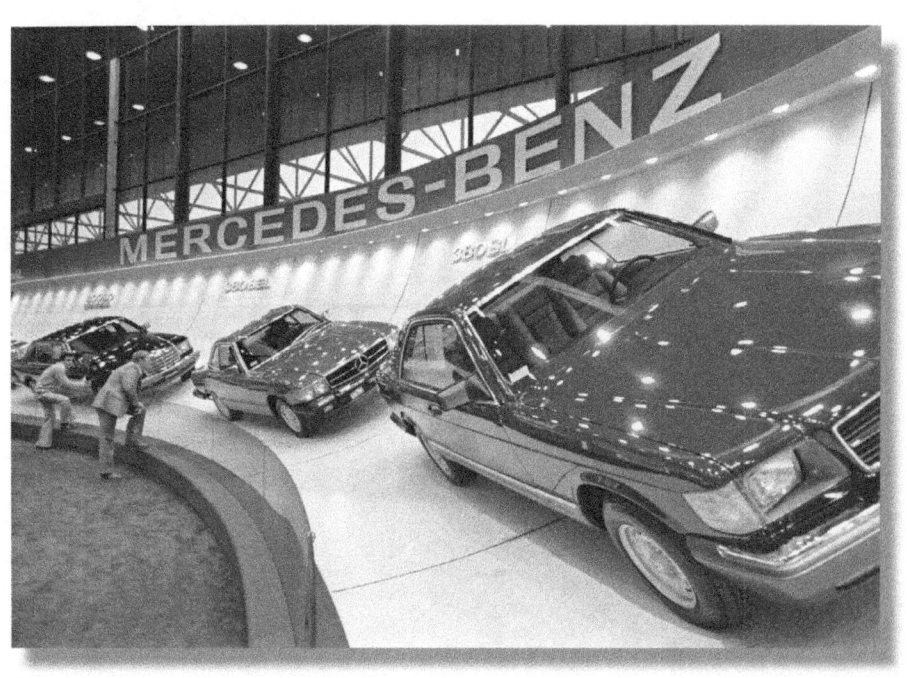

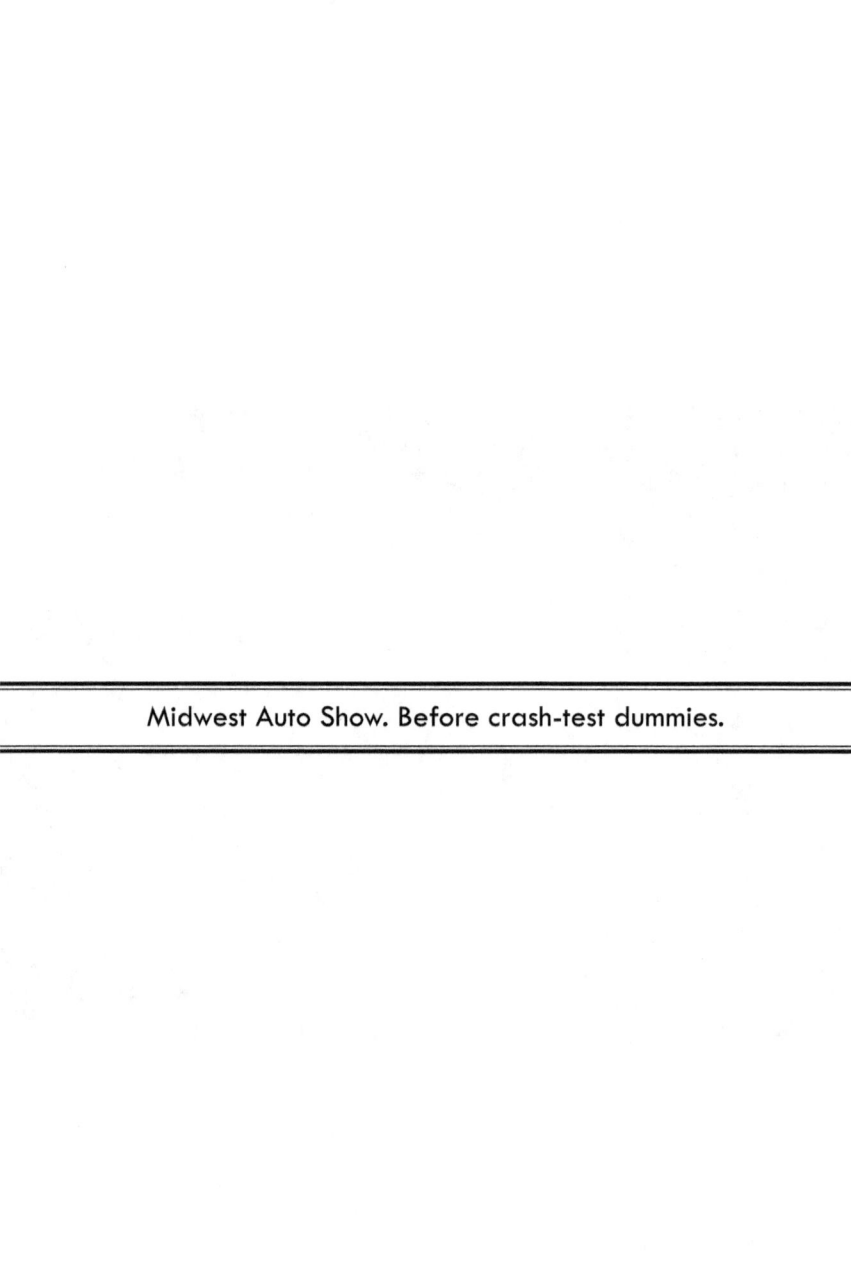

Midwest Auto Show. Before crash-test dummies.

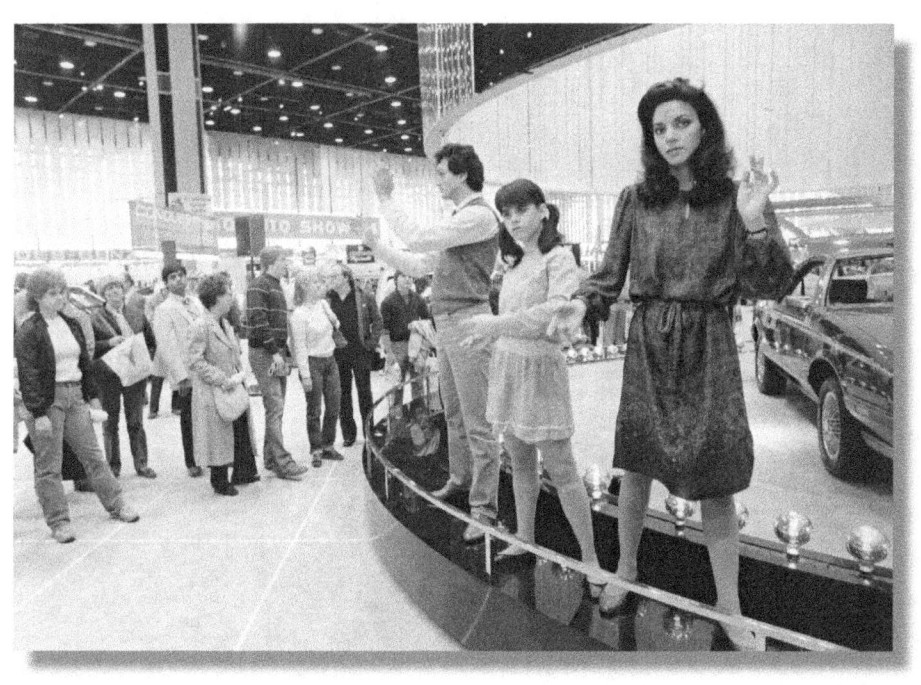

Yup, she makes me think of pipe connectors. Won't forget that.

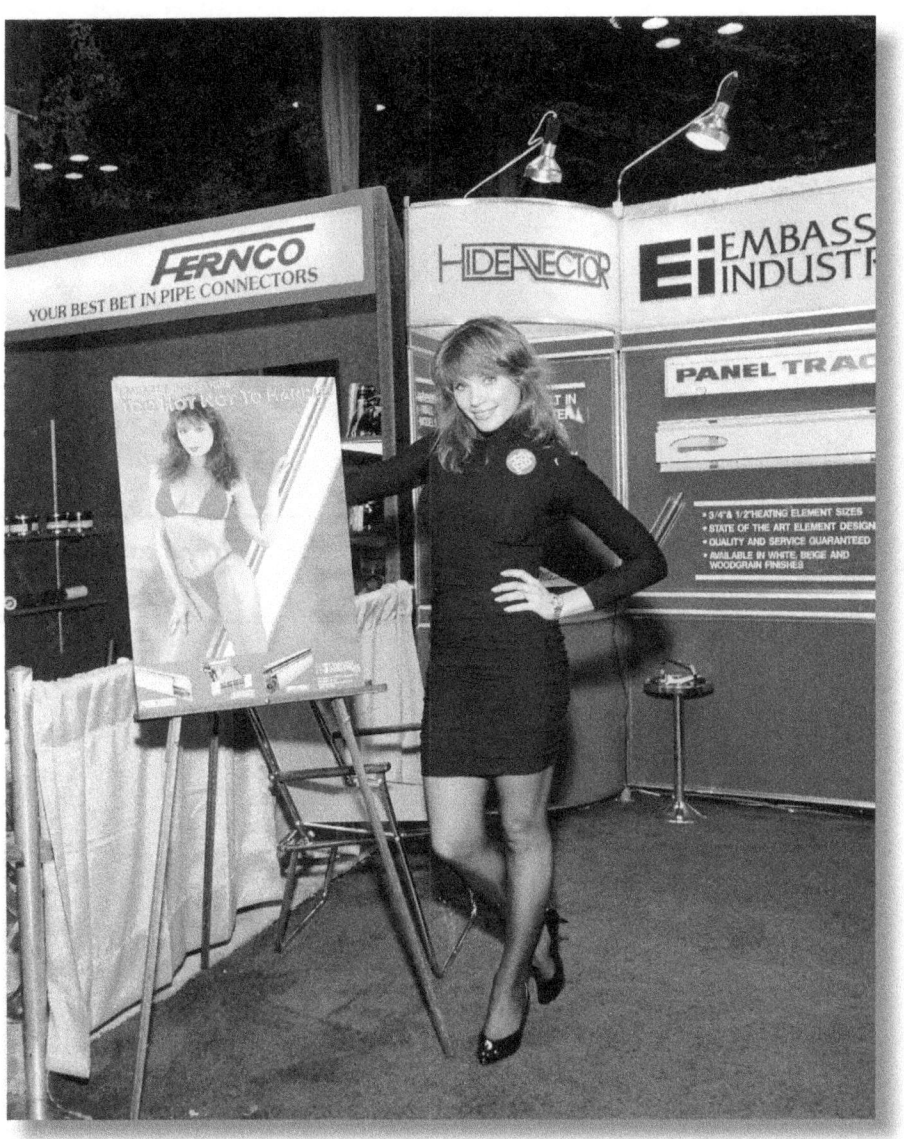

Tri-State Hospital Show. *This thing has more uses than you can imagine. Like hiding this coat.*

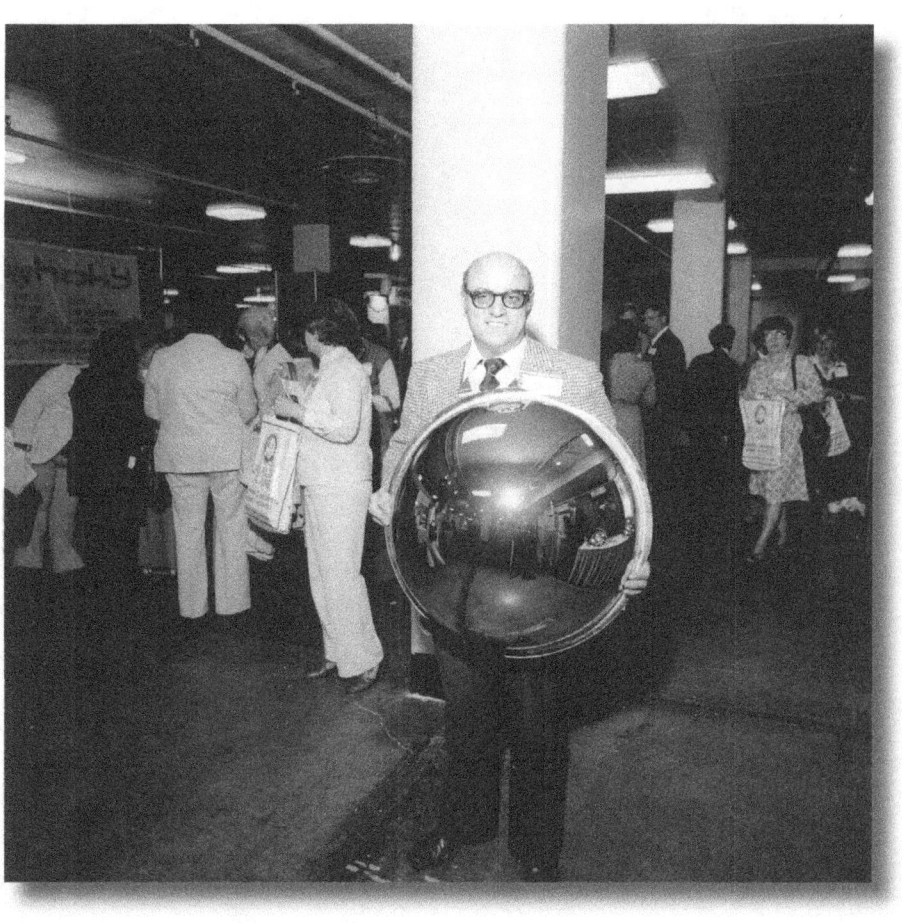

Graph Expo. Class in session. We teach. You buy.

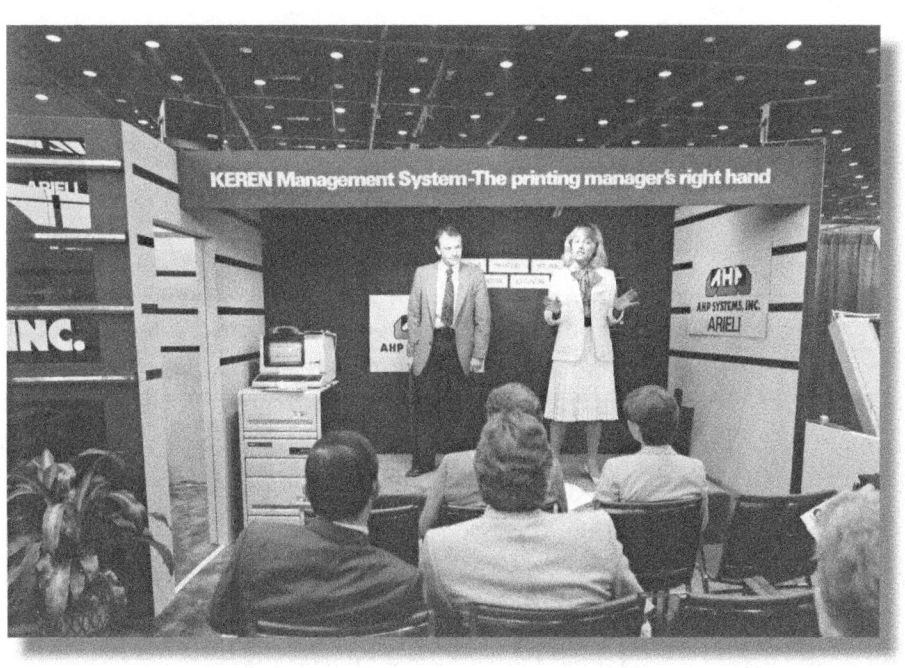

Materials Handling Show. *Your men won't hesitate
when it's time to ride this lift. Operator not included Gentlemen.*

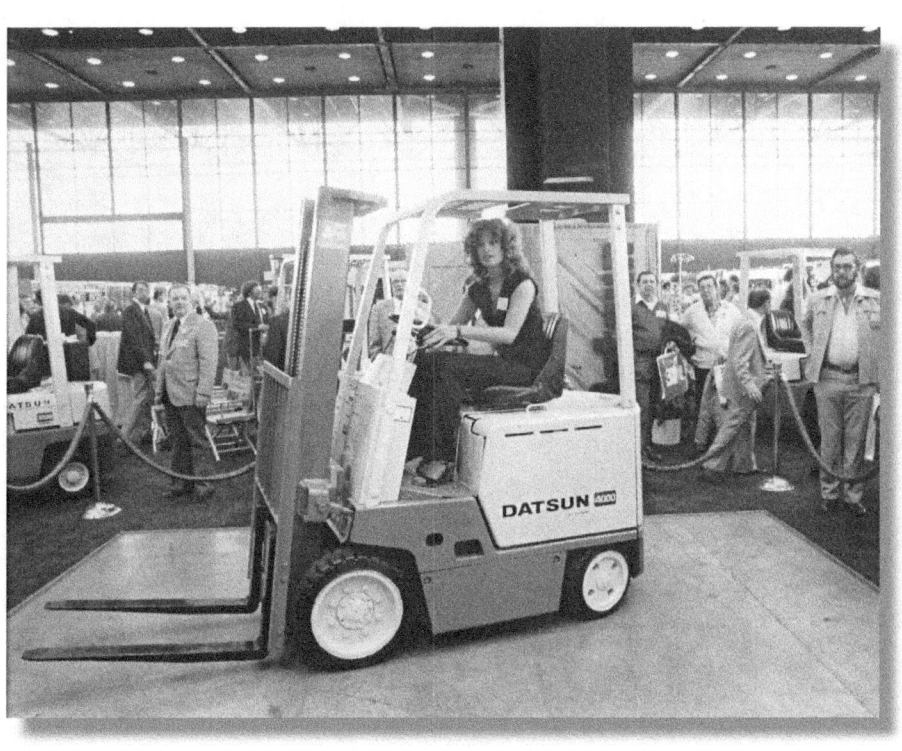

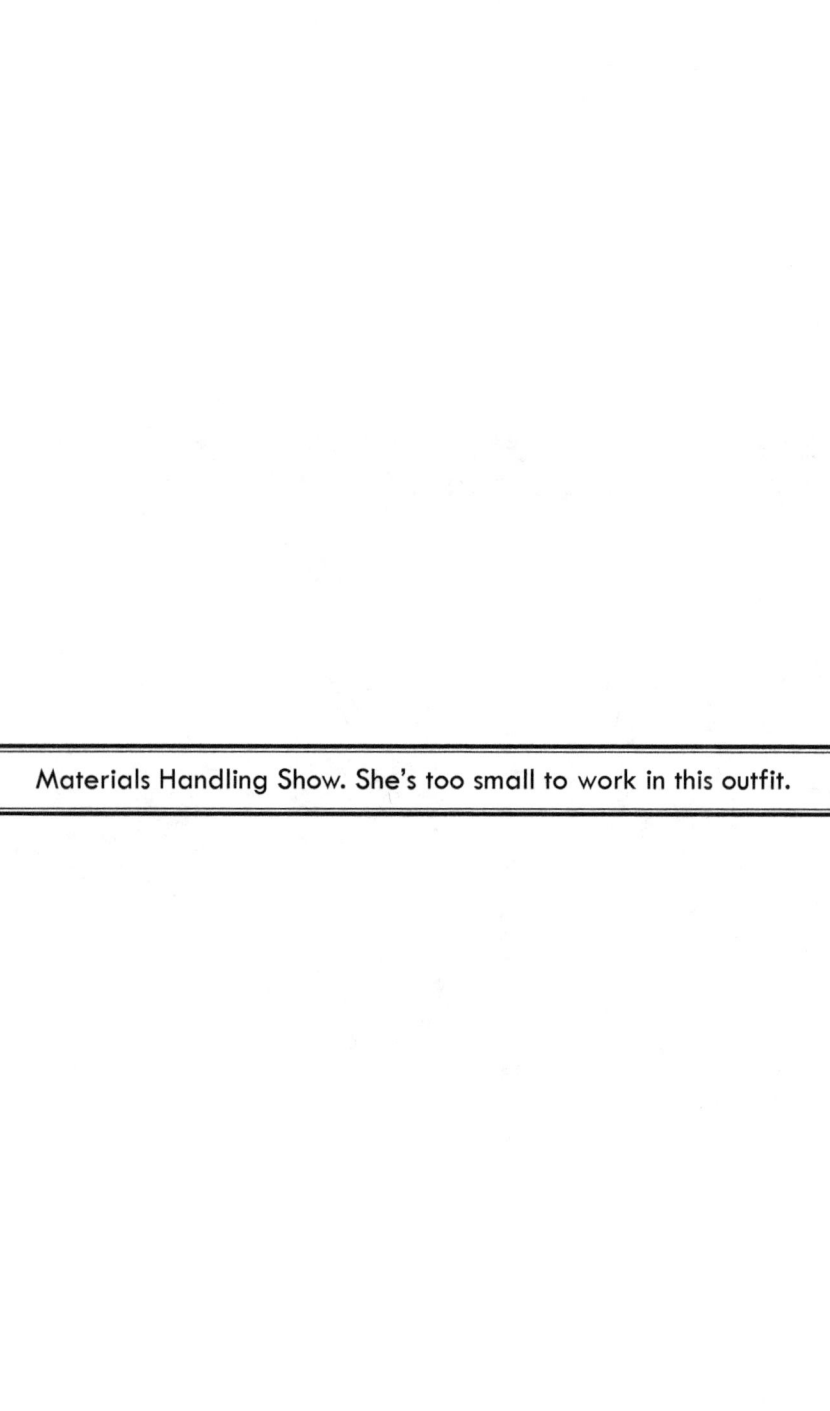

Materials Handling Show. She's too small to work in this outfit.

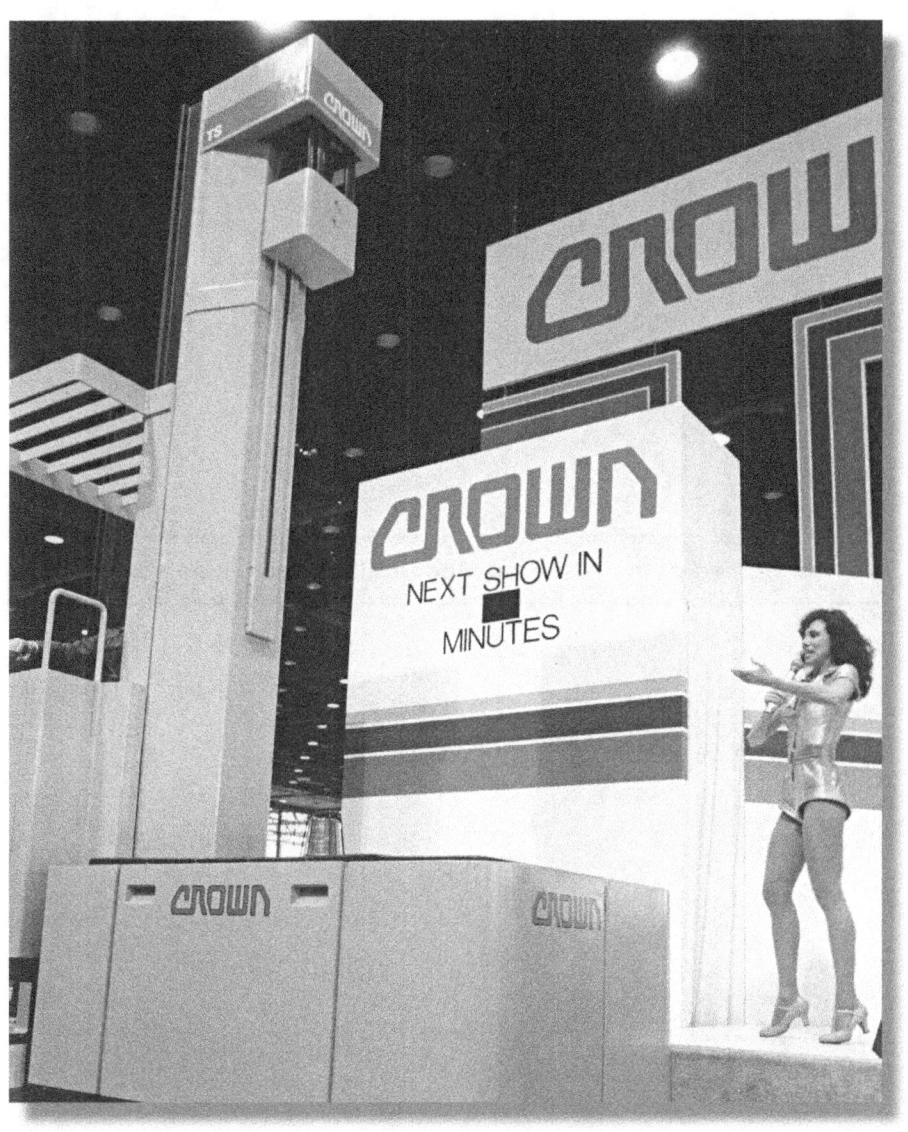

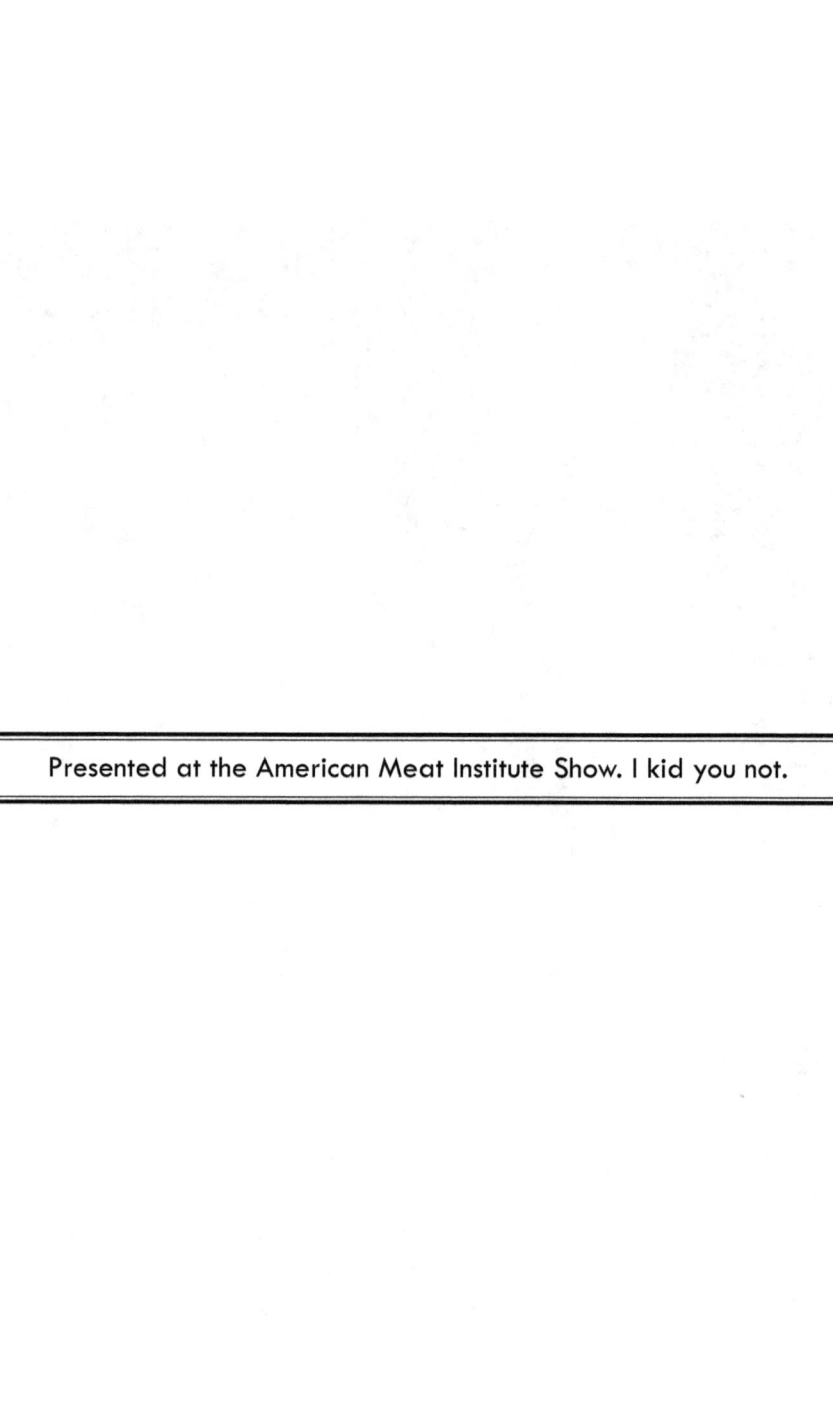

Presented at the American Meat Institute Show. I kid you not.

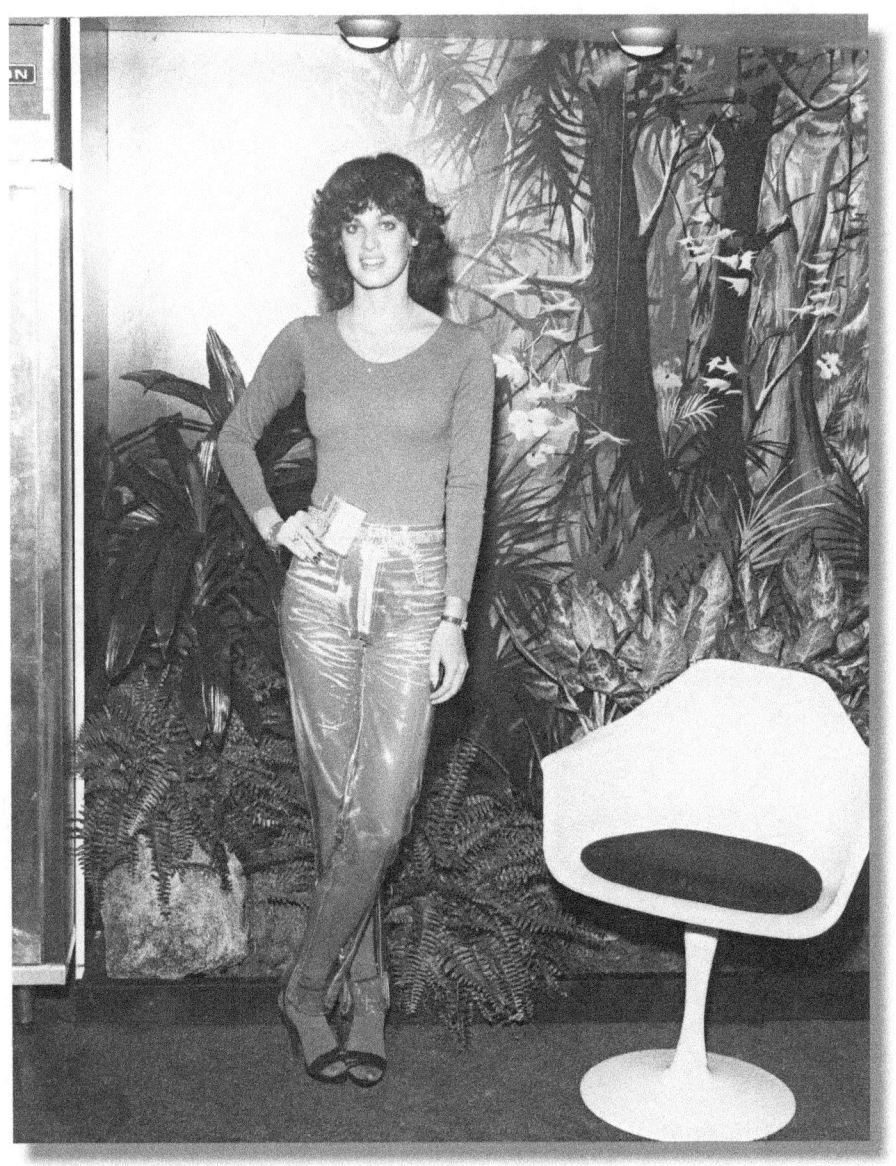

Mining Show. What do you think those guys are paying attention too?

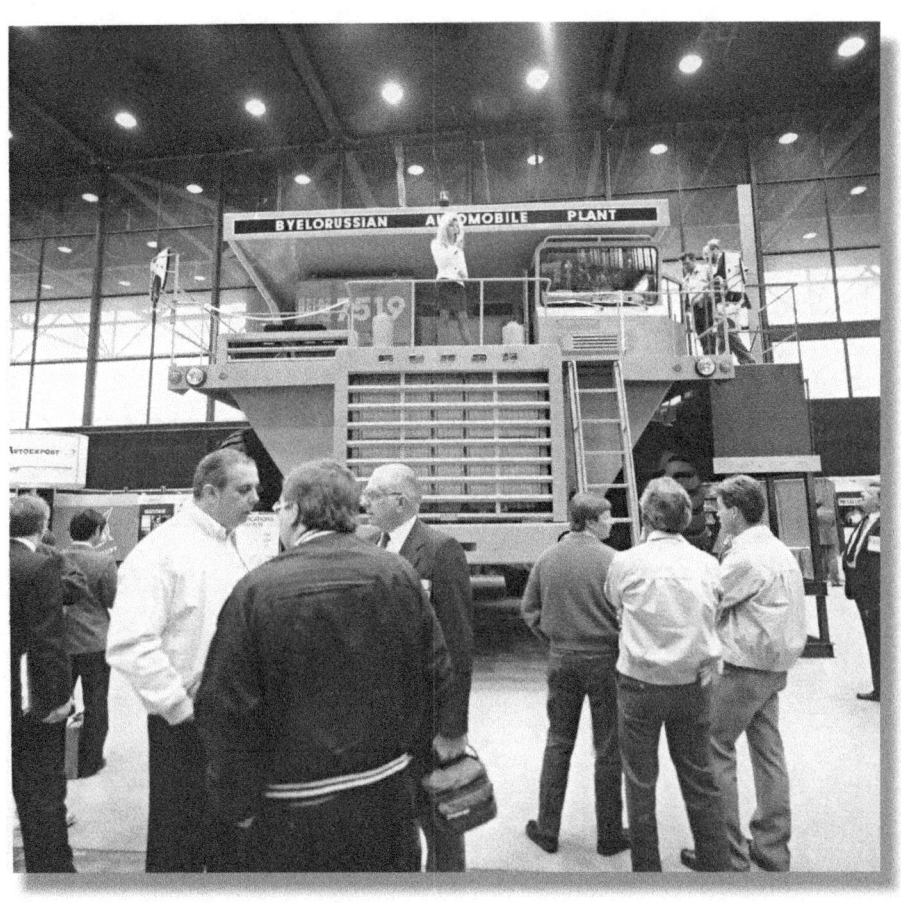

Materials Handling Show.
Bob, that's one fine looking piece of machinery.

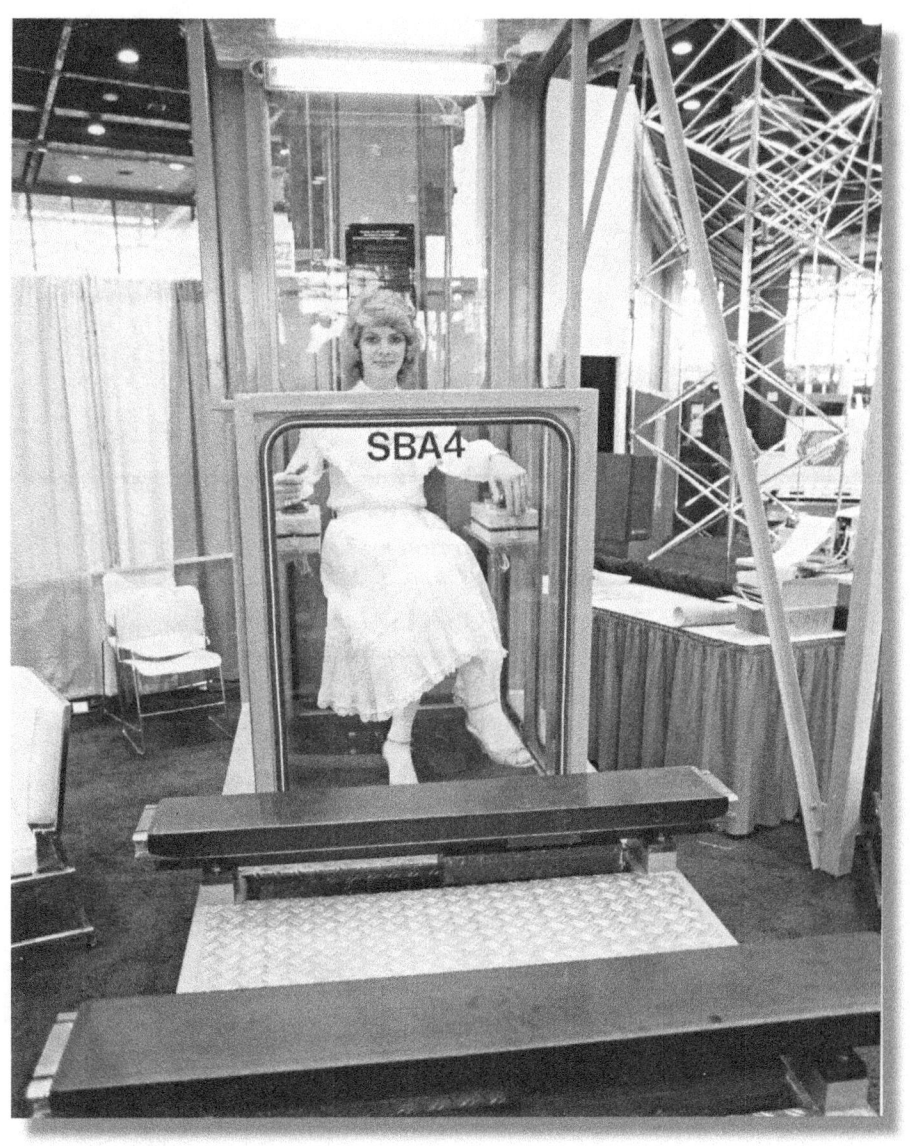

The Ryba Twins. *Buyer #1 Take your pick, Son.*
Buyer #2 Pardon me?
Buyer #1 I said take your pick: tea or lemonade
Buyer #1 Oh. I see I thought maybe.

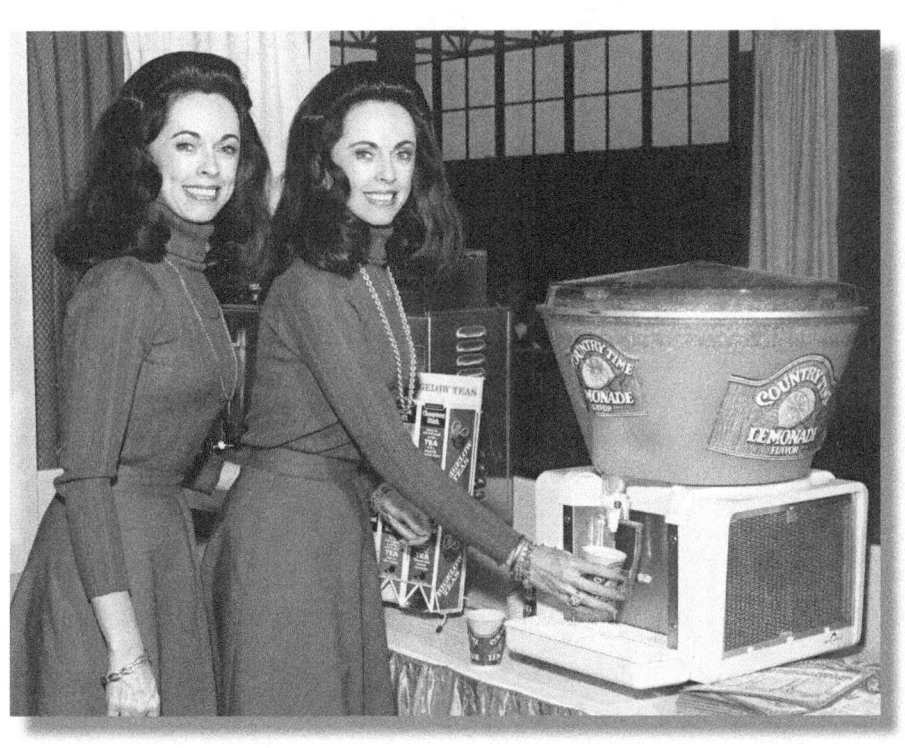

Radiological Society of North America.
I am not getting into this thing!

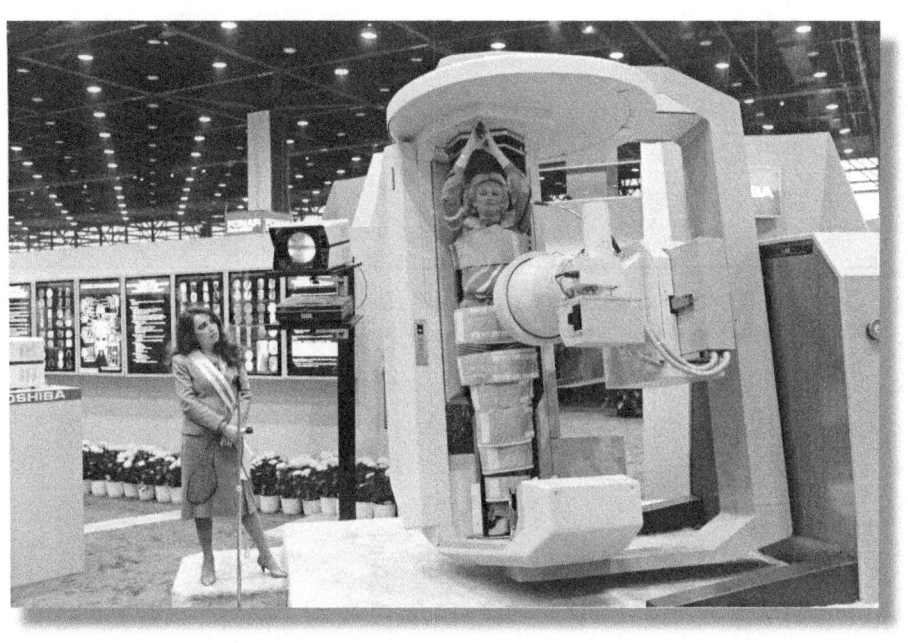

IMTS *Have a seat folks! There's plenty of seats at the back.*

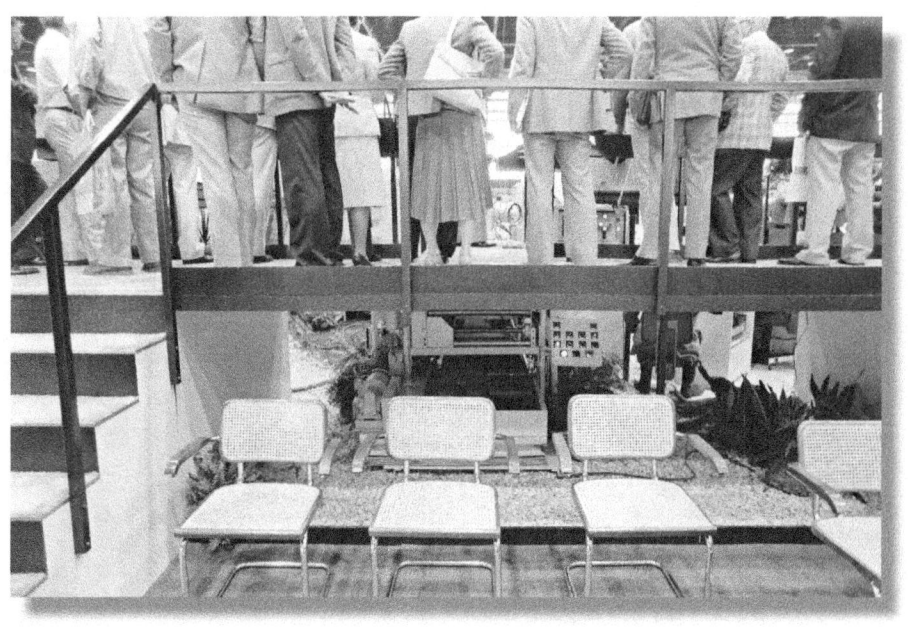

IMTS Psst. Hey Buddy. Can I get through here?
Which way to the Meat Institute booth?

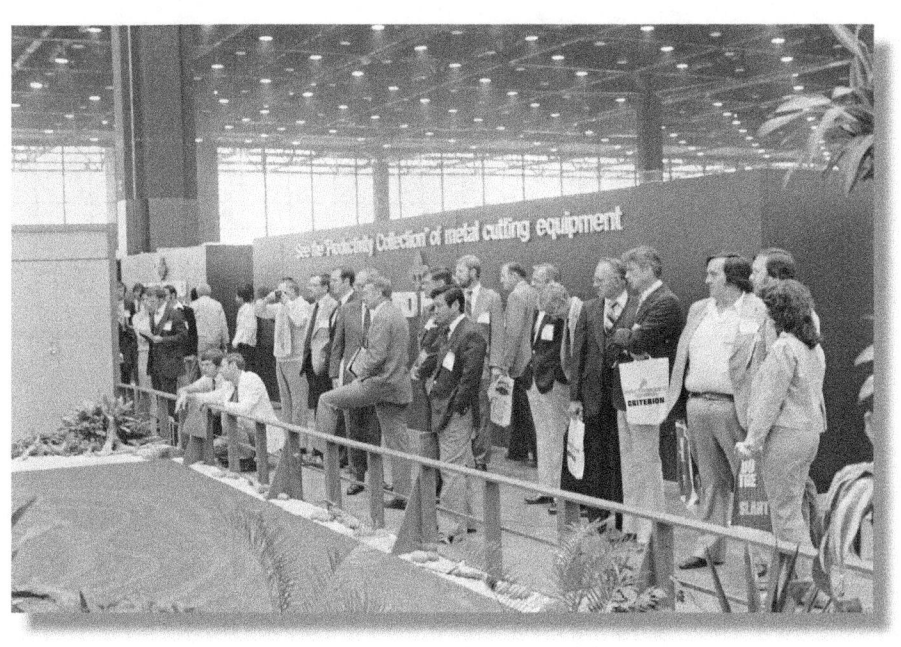

RSNA. *She keeps her distance from this one.*

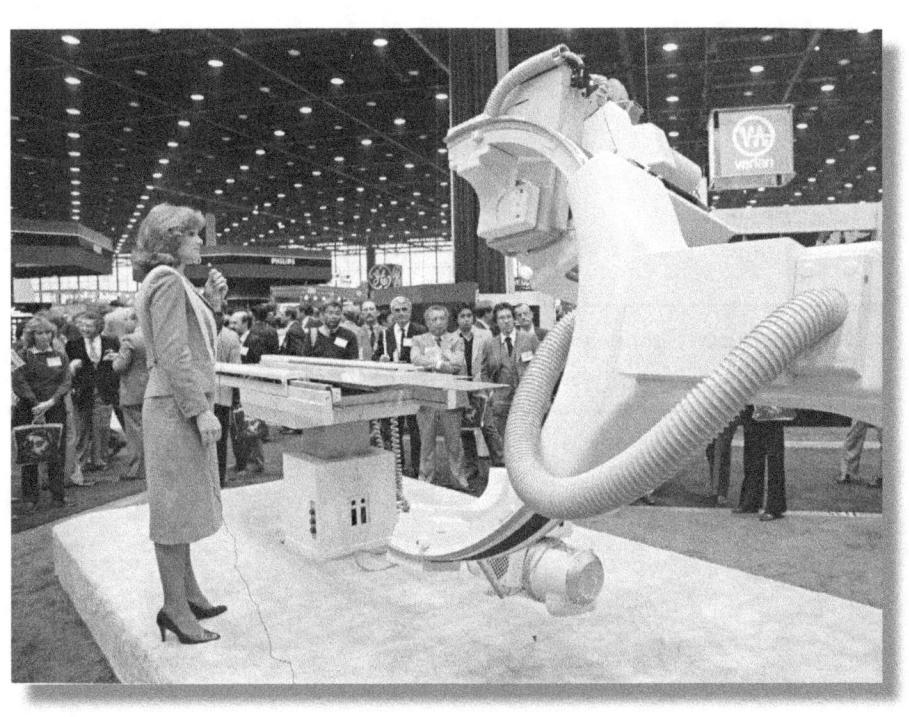

Graph Expo. *Gentlemen, I don't know how this thing works either, but look at what it just made!*

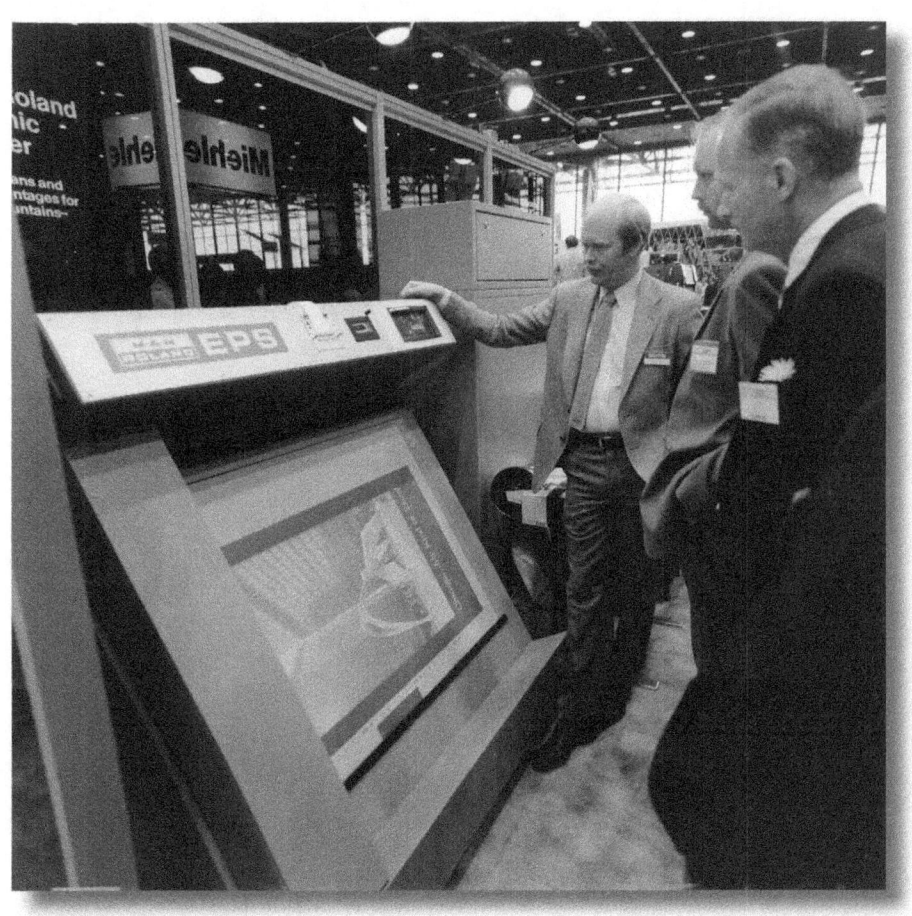

Golf. Concentrate on the golf ball.

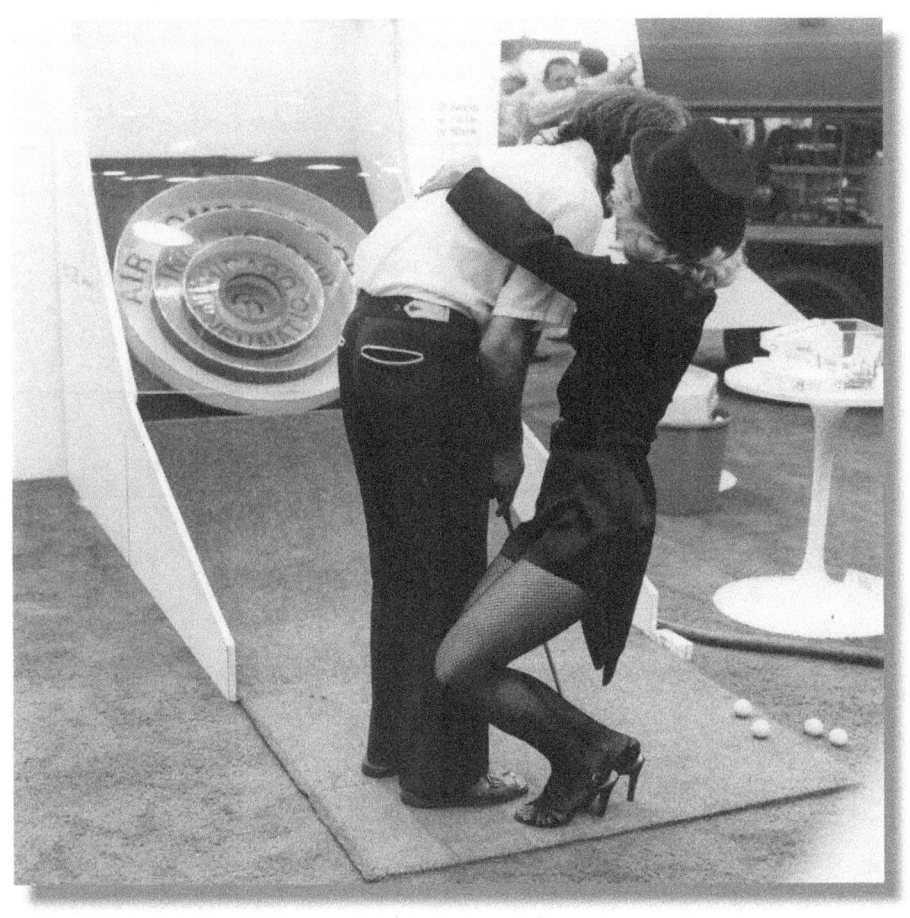

Design engineering show. You know,
I carried this sucker from Jersey, and I've grown kinda fond of it.

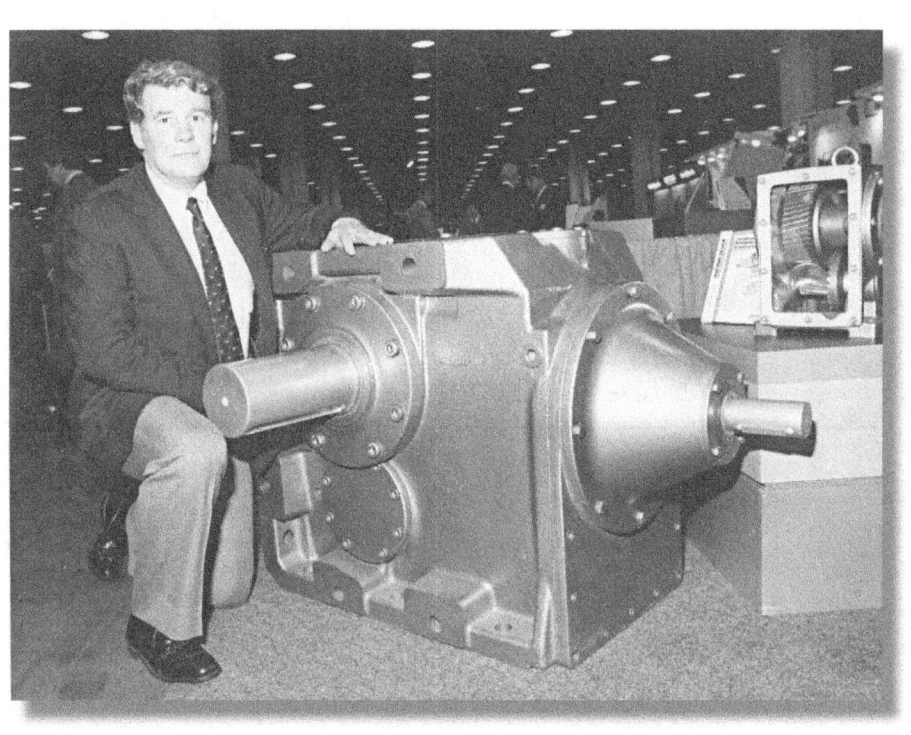

National Sporting Goods Association. Keep at it kid!
Believe it or not, that's how I got my start.

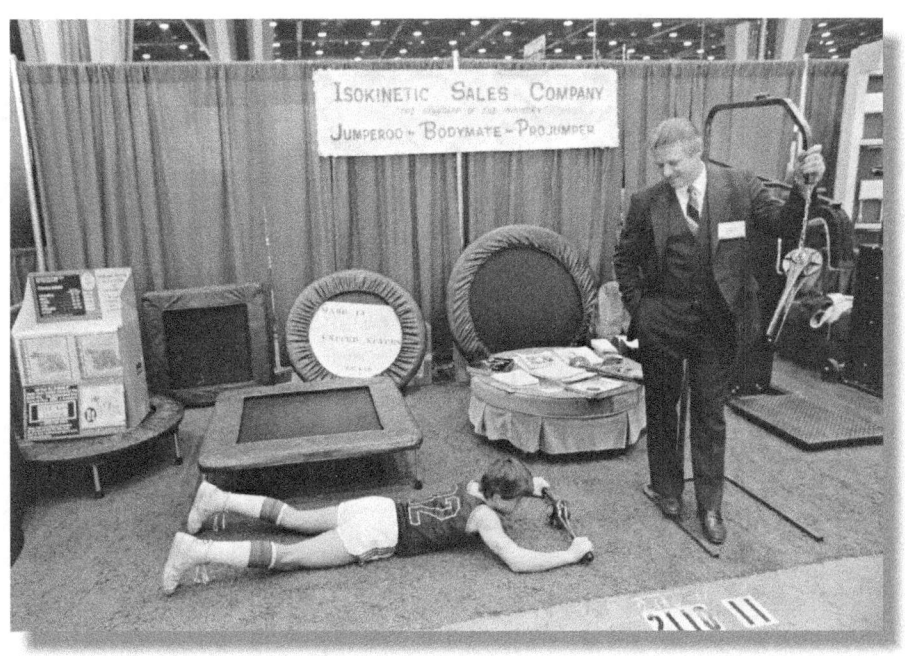

National Soft Drink Show

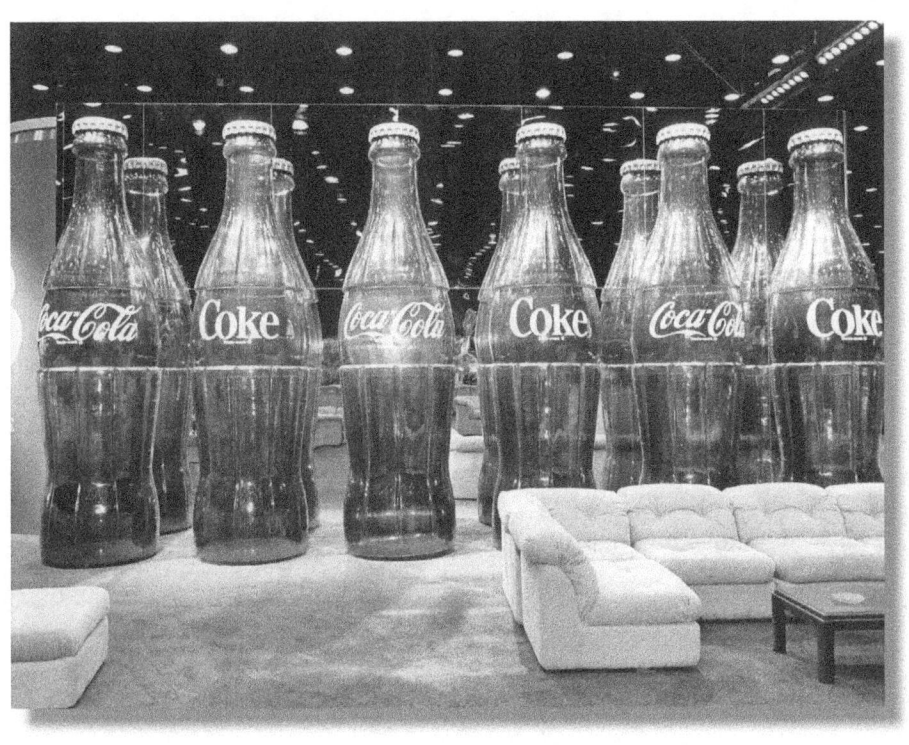

The Sale Ok Look. You take this baby home tonight,
and I throw in the free pocket calculator AND the poster of the American
Meat Institute girl. Deal?

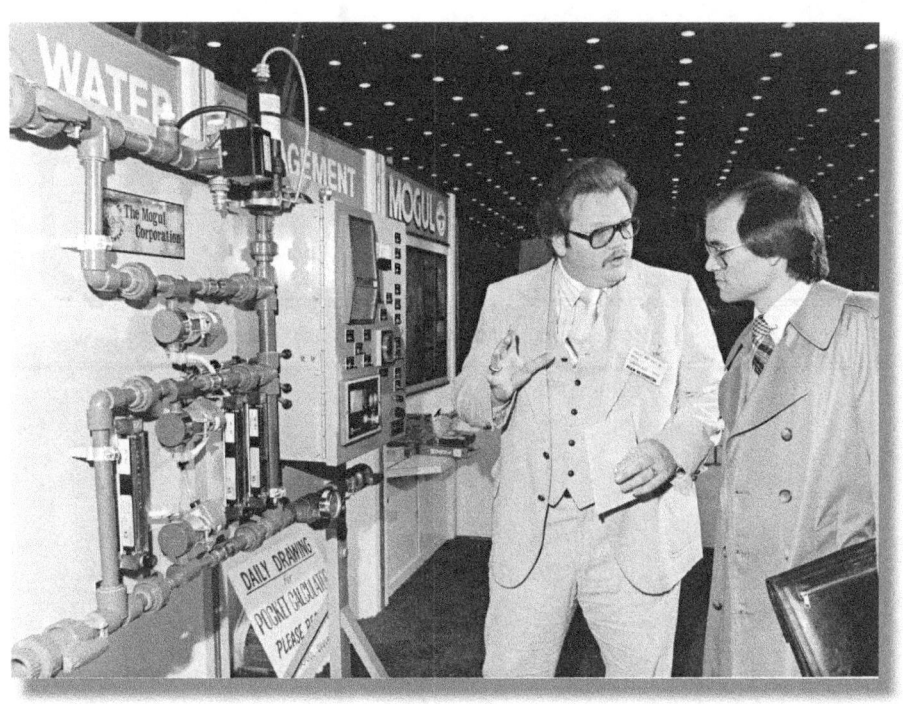

Shoe Show. And he'll do this all week.

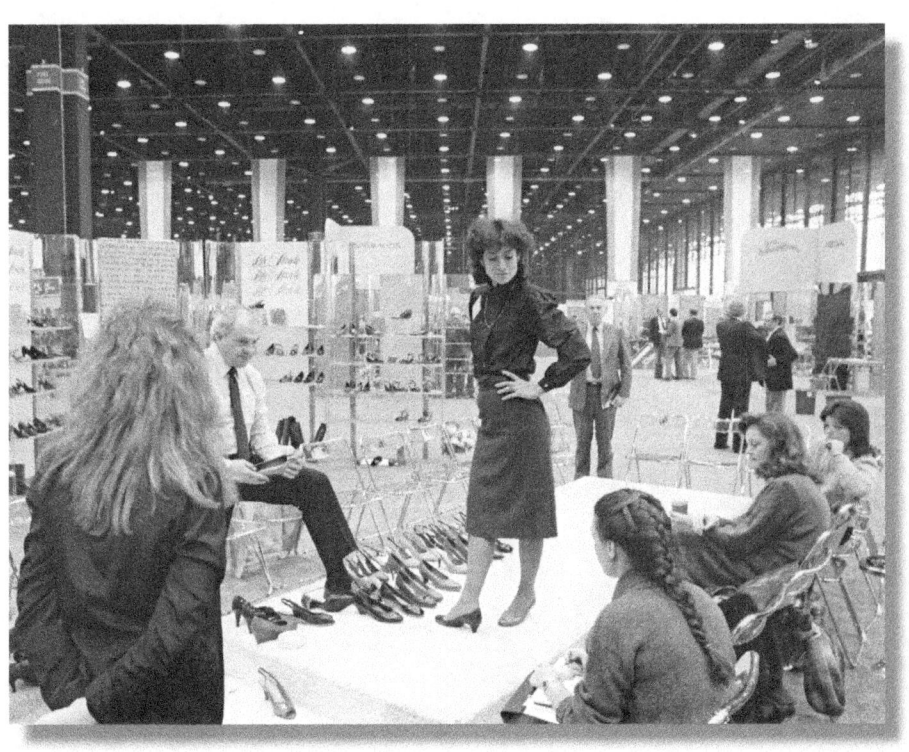

Did I mention that she's with the American Meat Institute,
and only the chair is plastic, Oh and her pants!

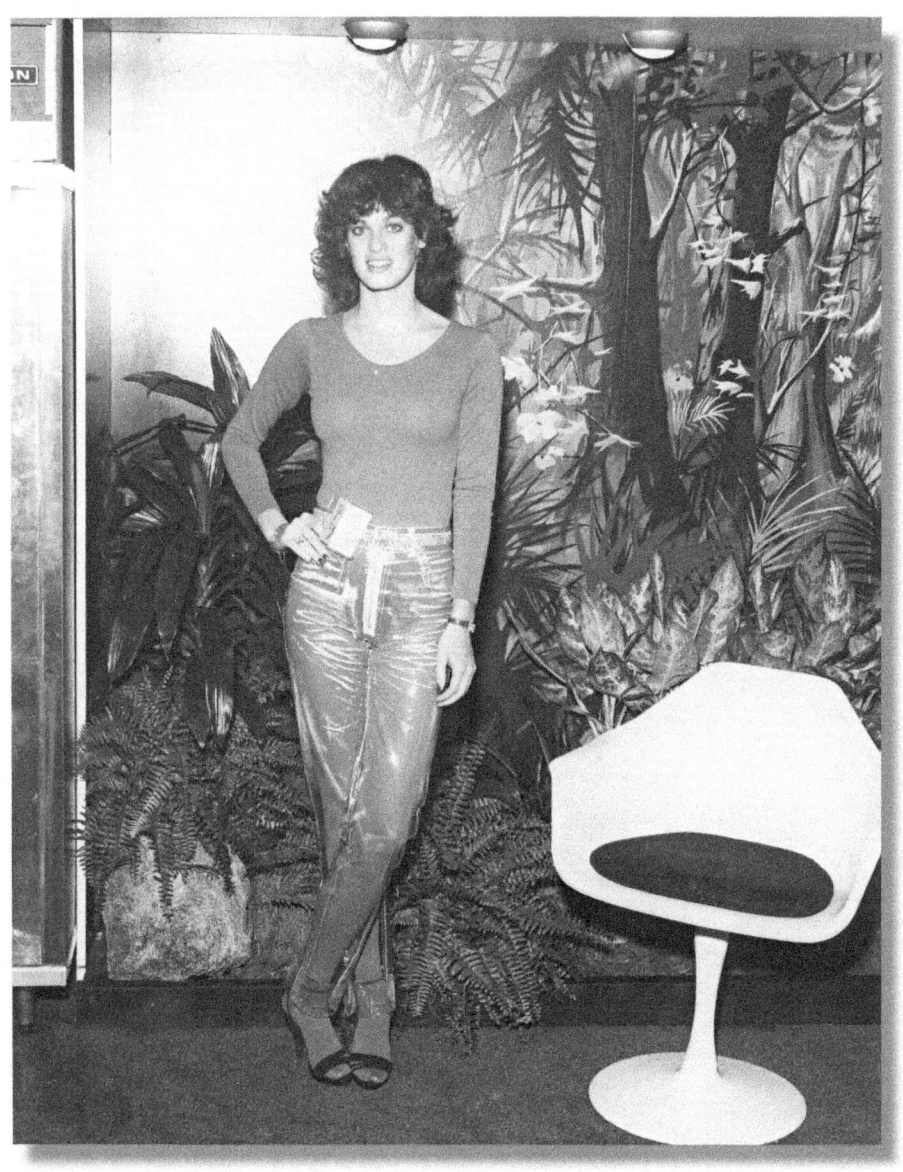

Build an exhibit in a week for three days of selling. Then tear it down.

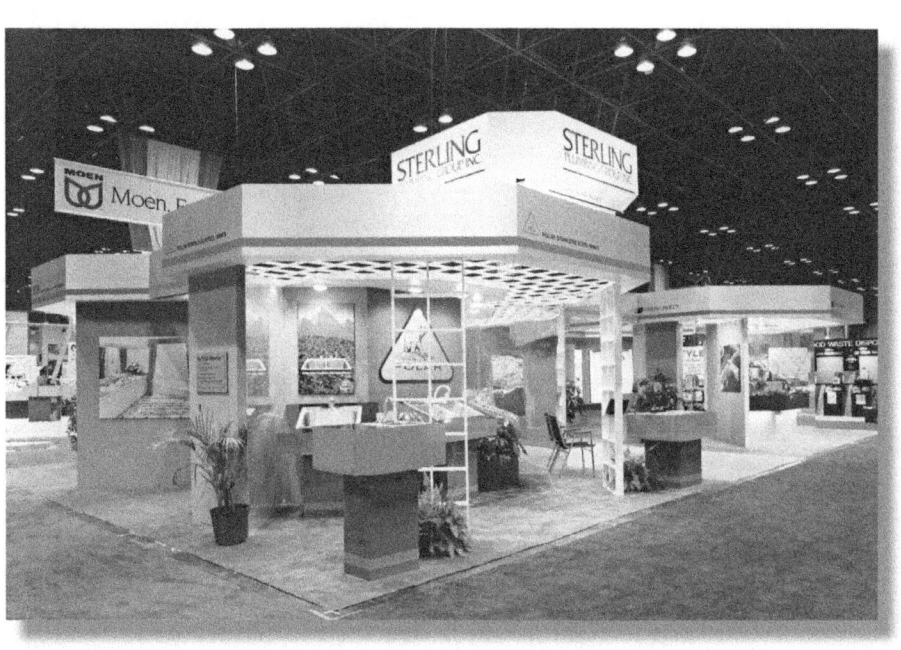

Transworld Housewares Show. See. I told you.
Our masks are comfortable AND realistic.

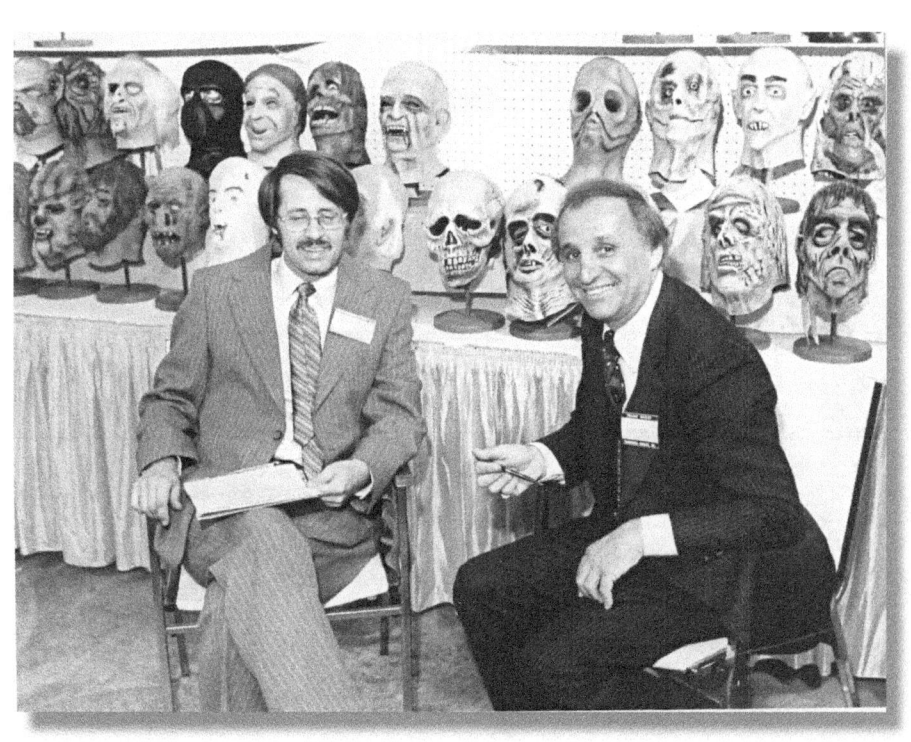

National Housewares Show.
There are few things they won't do to make a sale.

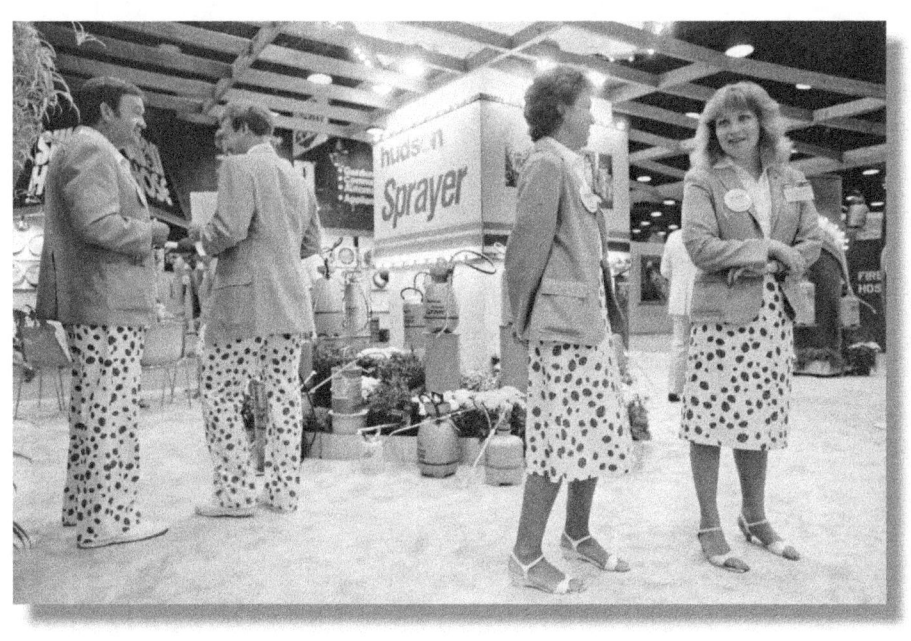

Topco / Transworld Housewares Show.
Notice it's nearly as interesting when the sex is so blatant.

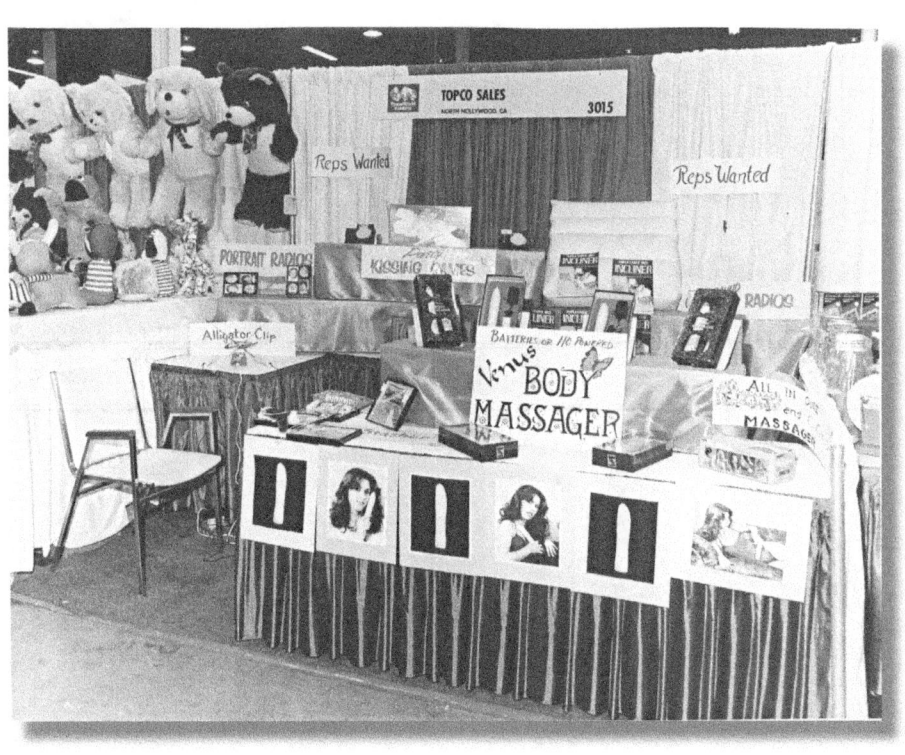

CES. Just because.

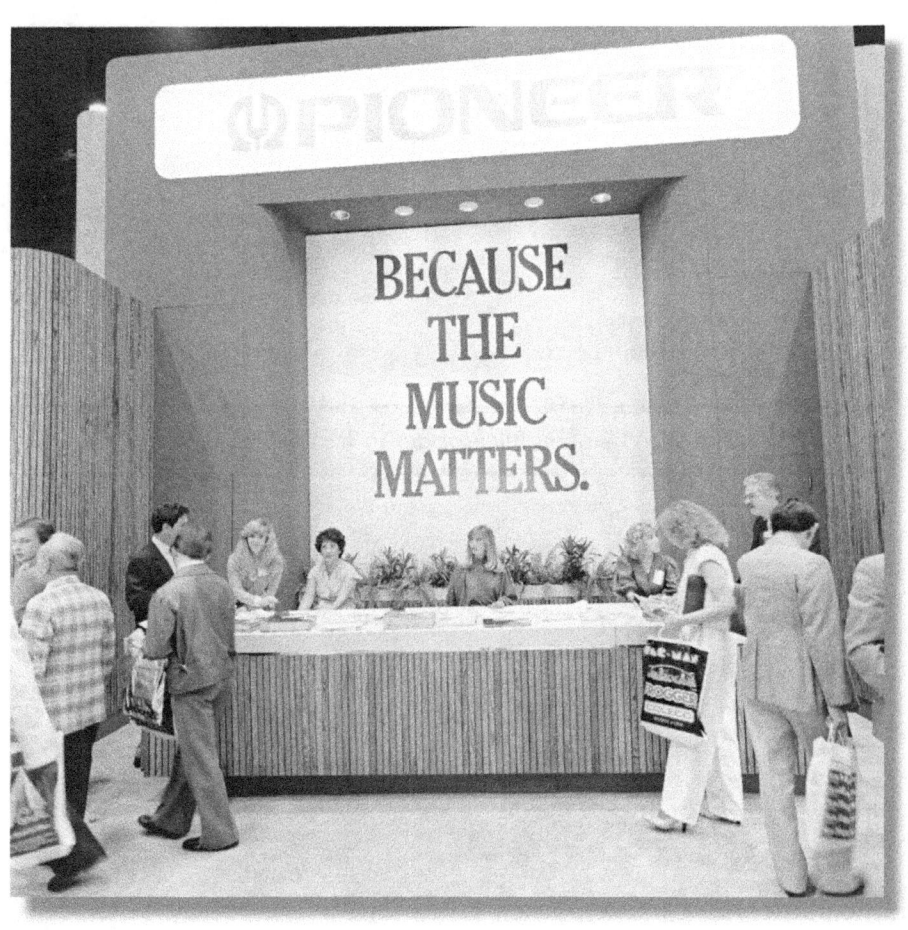

Beamscope. When you think about it. It's all a kind of magic.

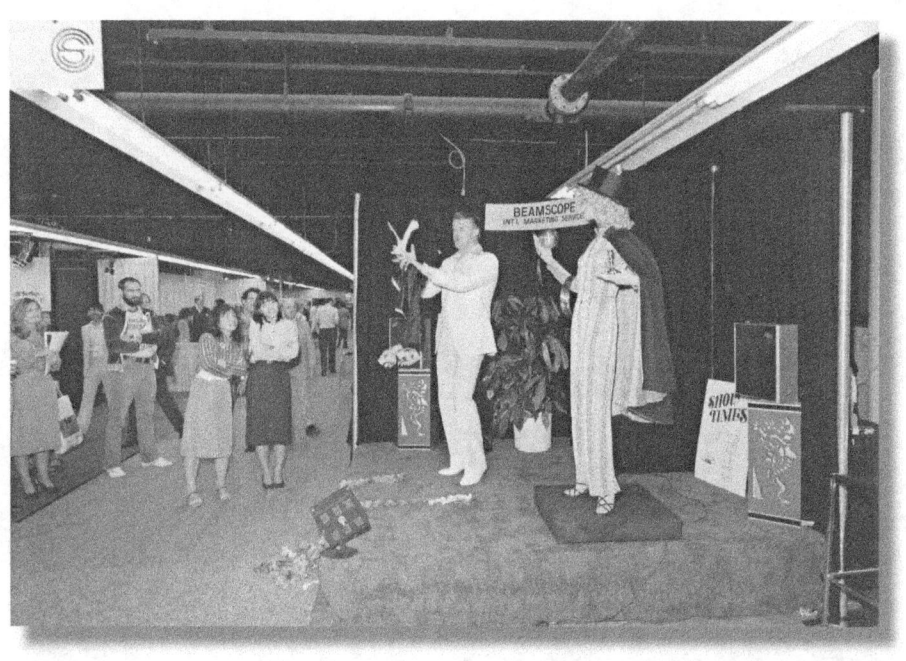

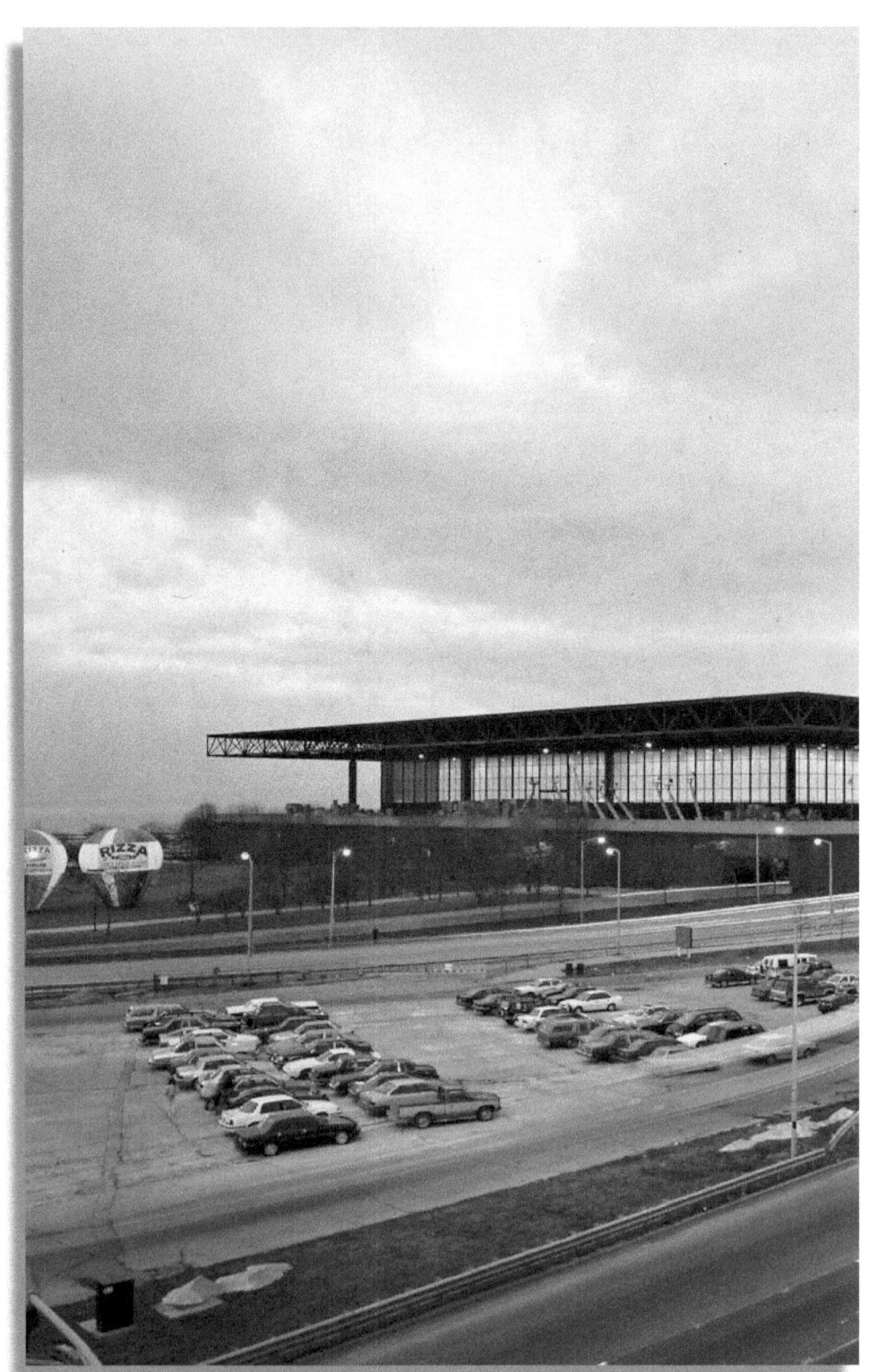

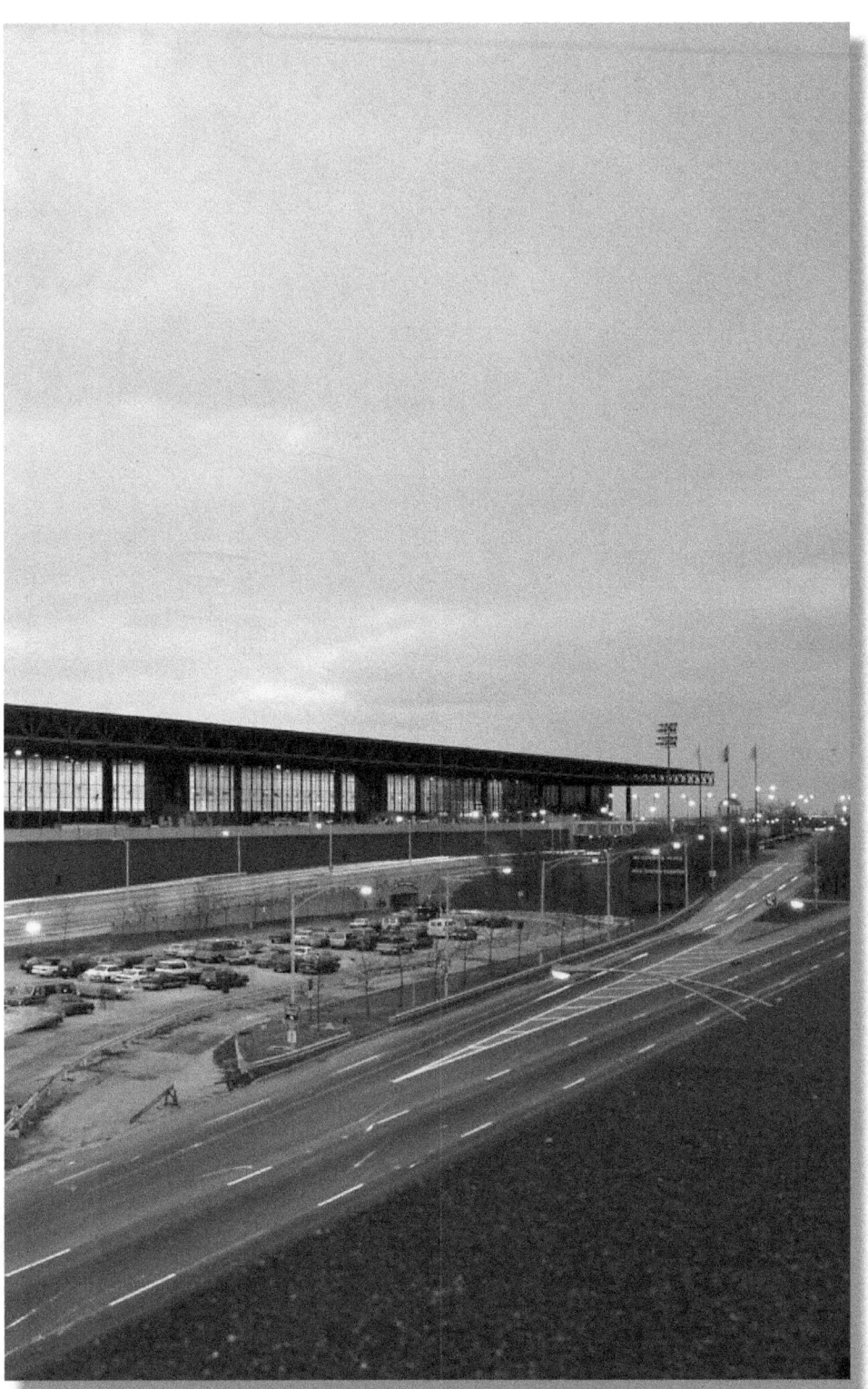

www.ingramcontent.com/pod-product-compliance
Lightning Source LLC
Chambersburg PA
CBHW071610170526
45166CB00003B/1038